SWING LOW MY SWEET CHARIOT

The Ballad of Jimmy Mack

a Memoir by

JAMES McEACHIN

Copyright ©2021 The Rharl Publishing Group

Inquiries should be addressed to:
Rharl Publishing
PO Box 5166,
Sherman Oaks, CA, 91413
or email beyondtheduty@gmail.com

In association with:
Elite Online Publishing
63 East 11400 South #230
Sandy, UT 84070
EliteOnlinePublishing.com

ISBN 978-0-578-84428-2

Printed in the United States of America

To Lieutenant Henry A. Schenk and to the blond-haired boy.

I did not know either of them well, but it was my great, great honor to know them at all. In combat, no one stood taller, they saved my life. They were two of the bravest men I've ever known.

And a special thank you to the people of South Korea and the manner in which they continue to respect and welcome the American Soldier back to their shores, enabling them to look back and see what victory has done for a great and giving country.

Swing low, sweet chariot
Coming fo' to carry me home
A band of angels
Comin' after me,
Comin' fo' to carry me home.

TABLE OF CONTENTS

Foreword by General Vincent Brooks 1

Introduction: A Band of Angels 3

Chapter 1: A Uniform to Wear 11

Chapter 2: A War to Fight...25

Chapter 3: A Jesus Figure 35

Chapter 4: It's Midnight Again...51

Chapter 5: The Ballad of Jimmy Mack 67

Chapter 6: The Silver (and Black) Screen 89

Chapter 7: "Hire Him, Henry!" 107

Chapter 8: Misty Watercolor Memories..121

Chapter 9: Swing Low, Sweet Chariot..145

Acknowledgments...160

Addendum A: War...162

Addendum B: Stars 167

Addendum C: Missing for Six Decades 173

Addendum D: Superman Talmadge 177

Addendum E 183

A Final Postscript...185

About the Author 187

FOREWORD

When one contemplates history, it is all too easy to accept that which has been captured in volumes as the full compendium of all that transpired. But as author James McEachin has shown in his gripping novels, plunging deeply into the unexplored depths of stories never told – and never forgotten by those for whom the experiences were more personal – there is more history to be discovered. "Swing Low, Sweet Chariot" fulfills this need in an extraordinary way. As it ties together the source threads of other works by him, James McEachin reveals the full tapestry of his life. It is "His-story".

From his rural North Carolina origins to his entry into the U.S. Army as a combat Soldier who sought to "meet the elephant" as veterans describe the ultimate test that is combat, and meeting it he did, etching his memory, even his soul, and circumscribing his journey through an adventurous, albeit tumultuous life. As James shares his-story a reader like me can feel the excitement of new opportunities imagined by James at each stage of his life and can also feel the pains associated with opportunities that turned out to be not so exciting after all.

Throughout his journey, James McEachin, like the protagonists in each of his novels (they are, as we learn, visions of himself through the prism of storytelling), demonstrates a very consistent attribute – determination. In my nearly two decades of relationship with James, aka Jimmy Mack, aka Keach, aka Jim, all of whom the reader will meet in the pages of this book, I have repeatedly been inspired by his determination. It is no wonder, he who is in his 80's at the time, could memorize the lines of a one-person play, fly for almost 20 hours to the Middle East, and perform in front of a group of troops who, while separated in age by three to four generations, immediately connected with the character. Those were my troops, and I was there to witness this uncanny power. Years later, at nearly 90 years old, James came to Korea where I escorted him to a position in the restive De-Militarized zone of Korea overlooking the very place where the permanent etching on his memory and soul occurred sixty-five years earlier. He was determined to return there in search of what had been lost, only to find fragments of that portion of his tapestry.

I encourage the reader, regardless of generation or gender or ethnicity, to read this as not only James, now over 90 years old, telling his-story, but as a chronicle of global change and societal impact. James McEachin was on the front lines, in each of his manifestations. And now, he is giving us a chance to hear perhaps his final story, lacking only the final chapter of his life that remains to be written.

Vincent K. Brooks

General, U.S. Army (Retired)

A fellow veteran of, and a friend to James McEachin

James and General Vincent K. Brooks at his command headquarters in Afghanistan

INTRODUCTION

A BAND OF ANGELS

I was born in Rennert, North Carolina, I had no friends and less neighbors. When I was just a child around the age of three or four my grandmother Becky would wearily move along in the cotton fields with a burlap bag filled the little, white, puffy balls of cotton dragging behind her. A determined and creative woman, her hair braided, my grandmother refused to be "boxed in" nor would she allow her long-gone friends or family to define her history. My grandmother was set in her ways and her eccentricities deserve to be mentioned; after all, who but her would think about singing opera while picking cotton. Nothing would ever replace the Negro spirituals, but she gave it a try, actually more than a try. She had a refined aura. I do not know if she was a good singer or not, as a child, I didn't know the difference. I heard she had a good stage presence, whatever that meant at the time.

My 5th grade teacher, Miss Nellie Parker, whom I got to know years later after we left the South and landed in Hackensack, New Jersey reminded me of Grandma Becky. Unfortunately, I didn't keep in touch with my grandmother after moving to New Jersey. But I did manage to stay in touch with a few people from my later years and discovered after getting out of the service that Miss Parker had ended up in Baltimore. I visited her then and once again, years later, when I appeared at the Kennedy Center in DC. Whether my former teacher knew how fond I was of her is hard to say, but she got the message when she had the occasion to travel to California to visit relatives. When I learned of her trip, I arranged for her to be picked up and attend a VIP luncheon at Universal Studios honoring Dr. Henry Kissinger. (He was very fond of Universal Studios and the people running it and would visit periodically.) Miss Parker couldn't believe who was sitting with her or the celebrities who were dropping by the table. She was quiet as all the celebs stopped or walked past. But then, she placed her hands over her mouth and watched intently as a big, burly man walked through the door and past the table. It was Raymond Burr, star of the hit series *Ironsides*. In shock, she whispered, "He can walk!" It then occurred to me, Ray played the handicapped character Chief Robert Ironsides on television and was never seen without being in that wheelchair and Miss Parker didn't know it was just acting. "He can walk! He's been healed! The man can walk! When did all that happen?" My former schoolteacher was chagrinned, but later on it started me thinking about her and the cane she was never without.

Visions of Grandma Becky, singing and working the cotton fields often come to me throughout life. As I grew older and began to learn a few things, songs would come to me and in turn, trigger another memory. Usually, I just let the memory go and continued with whatever I was doing. But this time, something was about to happen that would not only cause me to bring to mind my grandmother's songs and images of a nodding cotton field but would cause me to grow more introspective about where I'd come from. I can only assume she knew the power of songs and that they contained some sort of timeless memory. "Swing Low" was "colored" and dated back to the days of slavery, as did the old reliables, such as, "Take Me to the Water," "Go Down Moses" (my personal favorite), "Jesus Loves Me," "Onward Christian Soldiers," "Amazing Grace." But more than a hymn in grandmother's repertoire, "Swing Low", also prophesied the angels that would become so prominent in my life. Saving me, I believe, from an early life trapped in tiny Rennert, North Carolina, from an early death on more than one occasion, and most of all, from becoming just another "colored" whose time would be cut short by unfortunate circumstance. Unknowingly she was preparing me for what was further down the road. I bet she wanted to say, or maybe she actually said, "Being colored is a privilege only a few people can understand. It don't hinder you. It helps you." My grandmother was the love of my life.

It was Monday, May 25, 2020, and I was headed home at the end of an unremarkable day. I had been living in Los Angeles for far longer than I had ever expected. It was late afternoon, and it had been a relatively calm and lazy day and I was driving westbound on the Hollywood freeway. There weren't but a handful of cars on the road and for once nobody seemed to be in a hurry. I popped on radio station KGFJ. It was the only black-owned and operated AM radio station in town and, in a sense, one of the few places you could get "hood news." They were playing the Coasters, an R&B vocal group who were infectiously singing about taking out the garbage and the trash, Yakety Yak. Suddenly, the voice of a female reporter on the scene interrupted the song to report on a fatality in Minneapolis, Minnesota. Out of breath, she made it seem like a national item and kept pouring it on. Sirens and emergency vehicles wailed in the background and the reporter, out of breath, went on to describe something akin to war. There was increasing urgency in her voice as she uttered the word race two or three times and the listeners learned that a George Floyd had just been killed and that he had been killed in view of witnesses on a Minneapolis street. Floyd was a black man. In alphabetical order, he was an Afro-American, a Colored, a Coon, a Jig-a-boo a Minority, a Negro, a Nigger, and a Son of a slave. Worst of all, he was an illegitimate member of the human race. Floyd was black, most of the witnesses were black, and Floyd, was killed in a black ghetto-setting the stage for an explosion of outrage. The stage was set and without wasting a second, this man's blackness was already being used to both justify and condemn his death at the hands of a white police officer. My grandma's rising and falling voice hummed in my mind.

My thoughts jumped back to 1965, when I observed firsthand the Watts Riots – a riot sparked by the arrest of Marquette Frye and accusations of excessive police aggression. At the time, I was finishing up a recording session at Gold Star Studios on Santa Monica Boulevard. I remember that upon hearing the news of the tragedy, I got into my car and made it all the way to South Central L.A. in record time. I parked my car on 103rd and Avalon and walked through a familiar scene. I should clarify: It looked familiar all right, but not as a scene of L.A. It was a scene of war. It was battlefield-like, and I was there observing the carnage of modern injustice and its consequences when I was stopped in my tracks by a platoon of National Guardsmen. Their faces were obscured by shielded helmets developed for soldiers fighting other soldiers, not American citizens, and certainly not me. Their rifles swung in my direction. Another step and I would not be here today.

While I was considering the news in Minneapolis through the context of Watts, I began to have even deeper concerns. A lot has happened in the country since 1965, but have race relations improved materially in all those years? The killing of George Floyd gave rise to conflicting emotions in me. As a black man who hailed from Rennert, North Carolina, I am familiar with the ever-present threat that white men in power pose to black men. But I also viewed the encounter with the experience of a having been a police officer. There are not that many who can say that. And here, a confession; I, too, was involved in a police shooting of a fleeing suspect some years ago. I didn't actually kill the man, but I was involved. I have been paying a mental price for my participation in the shooting of that young college student in New Jersey for over sixty-five years. Now, hearing about the death of George Floyd at the hands of the police, those old feelings came creeping back into my consciousness.

Suffice it to say, never in all my training—whether in the military or at the New Jersey State Police Academy—was I taught to jam a knee into a perpetrator's neck and hold it there for over nine minutes. I was once a soldier and I had killed in combat, but I would never have done that. Such a slow, torturous, sadistic death is taboo even in war, codified by international agreements. Few soldiers need a law to tell them what is humane or inhumane.

I am not by nature politically driven and I have no axe to grind in that regard. I tend to view politicians all in the same dark light, grandstanding as divisive, and what distresses me all the more is that we as a society seem to be lurching back rather than striving forward. For that, I blame many individual failures but none more than the collective failure to rein in what is demonstrably wrong. What came into my mind over the following days as I learned more about the killing of George Floyd echoed the thoughts that I sometimes have when I remember the shooting of the boy in Jersey: Shakespeare's brilliant plaint that the fault lies not in our stars, but in ourselves.

I am Exhibit A of this simple notion that life is what we make of it. Mine has been marked by adaptation, acclimation, and self-determination, as well as luck in places. This book is about, a victory not of heroism but of coming to grips with life as an ever-constant challenge to be met and conquered. Even at this ripe old age, I still welcome new roads, new solutions, and there are new lessons to be learned. Always.

People tell me I have the bearing and energy of a much younger man. Well, perhaps so. Maybe it is because I nearly died—twice. Maybe three or four times. I don't know. But I don't sit around waiting to run out the numbers. I don't sit around waiting for tomorrow for tomorrow may not come. Others tell me my life is unique; I hear it so much I'm beginning to think they might have a point. All I know is that at ninety-one years of age I am still hungry, still black, and I still get a kick out of watching the powerful trip over their self-importance.

Around the time my television series, *Tenafly*, premiered on NBC, I received a letter after testifying before Congress, from Jack Valenti's office in Washington on Motion Picture Association of America letterhead that read: "My Dear Jim, you were a triumph! I need not expatiate at length on the reception you got. You damn near got raped which, of course is the singular honor that TENAFLY conferred on you. And thanks for your presentation It was mighty valuable. I am in your debt, as is the organized film industry. Tell me who you want killed and I'll get to work!" Sincerely, Jack. I'm sure he was joking, though with Jack one never knew. There are those whose achievements are so minuscule they are hardly worth mentioning and others so low on the totem pole or even inconsequential to others, but in the name-dropping department, just ask my good friend and favorite producer, Dean Hargrove, some are unknown, but some will ring a bell, step back and step up to the big board and hear echoes of John Wayne. See the lengthening shadows of Henry Fonda, Bette Davis, Sidney Poitier, Judge Will Ross, Ed Asner, Carroll O'Connor, Doris Day, Admiral Michael Mullen, General Vincent Brooks. And there is Bob "the Closer" Lange, Billy Bush, Billy Dee Williams, Steven Spielberg, Eugene Marshall, and Steven Bochco. There's Lew Wasserman, Clint Eastwood, Dick Colla, Grant Tinker, Bill Clinton, Tommy Lasorda, and Quincy Jones. These are just a few of the giants that I've come to know over the years. Many I worked with, some I consider friends, more than a few I have told to get lost. I, however, have grown beyond all that. I was lucky to have few enemies and whatever grudges and petty arguments I did have, paled before the list of friends and inspirations who made my life fuller and better. I should point out, in fairness, that not everyone who has known me has taken to me.

Now as I sit here at my desk, pen and computer notebook in hand, mind reaching back through the tides of time scanning the memories of my years on earth, I can say my story of war, of chance, of luck, of inspiration, and of gratitude. I have learned to weather the whirlwinds of life.

I am reminded by more factors than I can count, that life never stands still; that sometimes it seems to be hostile to the very existence of man. Right now, outside my door, a pandemic is disrupting the very rhythm of life, replacing it with tentative steps, fear, face masks, latex gloves, and disinfectant. And I wonder whether the long road of my life has led me into an abyss, or if perhaps, I have lived my life so as to be worthy of the time given me by the band of angels who have saved me time and time again. I hope the latter is true.

I would like to mark this project as closed, I have done what I wanted to do, said what I have wanted to say.

My Mother and Grandma Becky

CHAPTER 1

A UNIFORM TO WEAR

Today, many of the places from my childhood still stand in hidden little Rennert, North Carolina, looking something like wooden mushrooms on the flat landscape. The most impressive is the Open Arms Assembly of God Church, its clean white exterior walls and black split-level roof still inviting the town folk to services on Sunday mornings and Wednesday evenings. I suppose my mother and grandmother could have been found praying in the pews there, though I know almost nothing of them, and extraordinarily little of myself other than that I was a child cast adrift almost from birth, abandoned in all but the strictest legal sense. Only when I was around four years old did I learn that I was the fourth and youngest child of James Elton McEachin and his wife Anna Black. As a toddler, I had been sent to live with my maternal grandmother, Becky, after my parents separated. My mother bundled up my siblings and fled Rennert for greener pastures on the streets of Hackensack, New Jersey. Apparently, she believed I was too young to go, so she left me with Grandmother Becky, with the promise she would send for me when I was a little older.

My father had absolutely no interest in raising me and he moved out of state as well. I only remember seeing him one more time in my life, when I was nine and I had returned to Rennert to visit Grandmother Becky. She must have beckoned him to come visit his son. He did, but he never got out of the car he was riding in. We spoke for a brief time, about what I don't recall, then he was gone again. Forever. I do not know when he died. I never wanted to know.

The sights and sounds of early childhood are disconnected blips in my memory: The leafy trees that swayed in the wind, weaving in balletic precision. The wind whistling through the branches sounding like violins. The railroad tracks were laid out arrow-straight, as far as the eye could see. My strongest memories are of Grandmother Becky's house on a parcel of land in the woods behind the cotton fields. It was no more than a forlorn shack, but it was my world, and only later in life did I wonder how a woman who didn't work was able to live in it. Not incidentally, perhaps, the owner of the land and house was around a lot. He was a middle-aged white fellow named Archibald; whether that was his first or last name, I don't know. I only knew him as Mr. Archy. A ruddy-faced man.

There was plenty I didn't know about Rennert. And plenty I wasn't supposed to know. I knew that Mr. Archy had a wife, whether black or white, I can't recall, it didn't matter then, but I do remember that they fought all the time, and that when they would stop, it seemed like she would sit and emit moaning sounds from every room in the house. And then she'd go into the kitchen and wait. With brush in hand, the little brutish man would follow up by coming into the kitchen just to spank her - a not-uncommon practice at the time.

Whatever the relationship was between Grandma Becky and Archy, and whether that had something to do with the crying wife, I can easily imagine all of them as characters in a Gothic novel by Flannery O'Connor, William Faulkner, or Erskine Caldwell, or a play by Tennessee Williams about the dirty little secrets of poor Southern folks. One could have described our place as God's Little Acre. Mr. Archy was later the inspiration for the plantation owner, Archibald McBride, in *Tell Me A Tale*, which I located in Red Springs, a real town just down the road from Rennert.

My grandmother was a wonderful person. She was saintly, and one of the nicest people you could ever meet. Much of the time, she allowed me to stray, to satisfy my youthful curiosity. I think she wanted me to grow up faster than most kids and she had me out picking cotton, shucking it, and stuffing it into a burlap bag slung over my thin and insecure shoulders. Conceivably, this might have netted her some small change from Mr. Archy. Funny thing is, I didn't mind it much. I had an excess of energy, and I liked being out, doing what I considered grownup work. Besides, I don't recall there being any kids around, so I had to keep myself occupied. I had no toys, my playground activity was to tie a string around a penny, whip the string around and let the little piece of copper fly off into the distance and then try to find it. I would imagine the trees talking to me, trees that at one time may have been used to lynch black people.

That was a side of life I didn't yet understand, though it was a part of my racial heritage. I realize that as a youngster Grandma Becky tried to make me happy, to have a childhood of wonder and discovery even in a wasteland like Rennert which is why I revere and cherish her memory. Toward that end, she understood that I liked to have my space, but I think she underestimated my precociousness, my impetuousness, my desire to want to go a step beyond the horizon—a trait that would get me into serious trouble more than once.

The first time it did, I was, as usual, alone, looking for something to do. I was padding around the scruffy patch behind the house we called a backyard. There was a pump that Grandma Becky used when she washed clothes. On a bench next to it stood a can of lye, which they used in those days to make soap. Evidently, I picked up the can, thought it was some kind of lemonade, and guzzled it down. I say evidently because my mind has blacked out many of the details of the incident. From what I was told, I screamed out, my esophagus feeling like it was on fire.

I fell to the ground, doubled over in pain, my hollering getting louder. I don't blame my grandmother for not warning me not to drink something without permission; it was just a dumb thing for me to do, regardless of age. I can imagine the horror and fear she must have felt when she heard my screams and saw me writhing. Her voice would quiver when she later recalled that I would have died that day had I not been whisked to what served as the emergency room in the county hospital. I don't know if Mr. Archy drove me there, but whoever did likely saved my life. So did doctors at that hospital, which didn't ordinarily tend to black people. I was later told they made an exception for a black child who would die within minutes if they let Jim Crow make the call. Gratefully, they didn't.

That was the first near miss of death's sting. For a while, I couldn't swallow much of anything other than a spool of thread I was given. That was to keep my esophagus open so I wouldn't choke to death. The hospital gave my grandmother a bunch of these little spools. When one was eaten away by stomach acid, I was to swallow another. It seems crazy that this was an actual medical treatment, but it worked. The event scared Grandma Becky enough that she decided Rennert was no place for a four-year-old. She called my mother from a neighbor's phone and told her the whole story. They decided I should go to Hackensack to join my mother and siblings. I don't recall who drove me there, just that on the ride I sat looking out the window, counting the white stripes on the road passing by. It was the first time I had been out of my little private world in Rennert, and seeing the buildings getting bigger and bigger, I was breathless.

Hackensack seemed like a teeming metropolis. In reality, it is a bedroom community in New Jersey, only four miles behind the craggy bluffs of the Palisades that overlook the Hudson River. Hackensack's population is only around 50,000 today, but that is almost twice what it was back then. And while it became a popular destination for affluent folks fleeing to the suburbs, Billy Joel said it best in song: "Who needs a house out in Hackensack? Is that all you get for your money?" Indeed, there was little suburban about it for us. My family lived in a small apartment, on First Street. It was in a unique-looking two-story house, owned by New Hope Baptist, the church that loomed up next to it. They were all eager to take me into the brood. My sister Alma was the oldest; then came the twins, my brother Verler—he hated that name—and sister, Gladys; then me.

My mother was a domestic, as they charitably called the black women who worked on their knees scrubbing white folks' kitchens. On a skimpy salary, she worked like hell to feed the family. She was always looking to improve her station in life, and soon after my arrival she began working in a factory called Curtiss-Wright Corporation that made airplane parts. It struck me that even in those new surroundings, things were much the same as down south in Rennert. The neighborhood was segregated. The schools I was sent to were all-black, cramped, too cold in winter, too hot in summer. But there were places to go and see, people my age to run with. None of us, with the exception of my brother Verler, misbehaved often. My mother steadfastly believed he would grow out of it, but until then, my brother was a no-holds-barred rabble-rouser, looking for trouble.

I had my moments, I am not proud to say, but I stayed on the right side of the law, if only to please my mother. We all loved her and tried to understand how much sweat she shed for us to have a better life. Not once did I ever hear her complain or curse her station in life.

She wanted us to breathe the air of optimism and accomplishment, but not to live in the dreams of the unrealistic. My concerns were those of a typical teen - sports, church, girls, the usual craziness of youth. Still, something was missing from my life, something undefinable. Without a male authority figure, save for Verler, who was not exactly a model to emulate, I was merely drifting. I needed a strong hand to anchor me, to give me a sense of purpose.

As if on cue, fate entered the picture. At Curtiss-Wright Corporation, World War II brought dramatic changes. After we reeled in shock and horror of that day of infamy, Sunday, December 7, 1941, the factory, like most others in the country, switched over to government contracts to manufacture essential parts for military use in tanks, weaponry, and of course, planes. My mother and her cohorts began working around the clock, riveting metal to metal. It was back-breaking work, but it brought our family up on the economic ladder, which was reflected in our improved living conditions. We moved to better digs in the "good" neighborhoods, first to 279 Third Street, then to an apartment at 190 Central Avenue.

In addition to new surroundings, our new station in life introduced me to concepts like dignity and self-respect. Alma's husband, my brother-in-law, was drafted into the army, and when he came home on furlough, wearing his uniform, it lit a fuse in me. Oscell Mann was his name and he hated being in the army. Like my brother, he was far too undisciplined to be a soldier. Fortunately, my brother was never inducted. I think he pulled a fast one to escape registration and service, but who knows? I, on the other hand, was dying to go. My civilian goals in life were to be a policeman or fireman.

I used to fashion makeshift uniforms out of paper. I still believed I would fulfill those dreams, but the uniform of a soldier captured my mind and most of my ambitions. Not incidentally, I had seen that women loved men in military uniform. A serviceman seemed to walk more purposefully, more erect, with more swagger. That star-spangled uniform could pay dividends.

Segregation in the military was a secondary matter, if one at all. In my limited world view, the uniform made all men equal—an assumption that would change radically as that view grew broader and as my intellect improved. Of course, I was still too young to fight in the war. I was only fifteen when World War II ended. But the aura and romance of the uniform only grew in intensity. I can recall how the city lit up when the boys came home after the V-E and V-J Days and were given parades down the middle of town, showered with confetti and adulation. When I saw those signs saying, "Uncle Sam Wants You," I swear I thought that bony index finger of his was pointing right at me. I had made up my mind to enlist, even though that meant I had to get my mother's signature.

I couldn't wait to register. My friend Emory King and I went to New York, got our papers, filled them out, and with a tad of trepidation, signed them, and waited. Every day I would wait—oft times I would greet Mr. Homer Dunn, the postman, by the P.O. box or beat him to his rounds.

"Nothing yet?" I would say.

"Not'chet," would come the unenthusiastic reply.

One day, my mother caught the routine: "Boy, what in the blazes are you doing botherin' Mr. Dunn for? You down here looking for mail. Who's gonna write to you?"

"Th' Army."

The wonder of it all was that my mother didn't object. She knew I was aimless, and the notion of me in uniform, subject to regimentation and discipline, was most appealing to her. The last thing she wanted was for me to be a layabout like my brother. So, when I told her I was enlisting, she was overjoyed. The war was over, and there were no life-threatening risks involved. School could wait. First, she wanted me to become a man. It was a vision we both shared; it was my business to see it through.

It happened very fast. After I was sworn in at the Army Induction Center on Whitehall Street in downtown New York, I and all the other youngsters inducted that day climbed aboard a bus for the trip sixteen miles down the southern shore of New Jersey for Fort Dix. It was August 8, 1947. Fort Dix was a huge encampment, covering miles and miles of barracks and fields; it was easy to see why it was the major depot for basic training. I was assigned to Company K, 24th Infantry Regiment, or the "Deuce-Four," as its men called it. The Deuce-Four was still segregated, just as it was during World War I, when infamously 118 of its troops were court-martialed for a mutiny in Houston that had been provoked by racist cops harassing the black community. By the end of the ordeal, eleven civilians, five policemen, and four soldiers had been killed; nineteen men of the 24th were executed; and sixty-three more were sentenced to life in prison. The continued segregation of the Deuce-Four in 1947 when I joined up was a perfect example of a uniquely American contradiction - asking young black men to lay their lives on the line for the ideals of democracy while being stuck in second-class citizenship status.

This would change, at least in theory, when Truman integrated the armed forces. But when I went on duty with the 24th Infantry, I was just one in a massive aggregation of black men like myself, some much older who had fought in the Second World War and had seen their blood brothers suffer pervasive discrimination despite the sacrifices demanded of them. Years later, my friend Tiger Davis referred me to -- Morris J. MacGregor's landmark work *Integration of the Armed Forces, 1940-1965*, in which MacGregor's meticulous research unearths more shameful instances of summary executions of black soldiers during World War II under the flimsiest of pretenses. To this day conditioned racism in the military still has not been put to rest, and military "justice," as applied by tribunals still infected by racism, is a compelling cause for many black veterans.

For me, however, in 1947—the year Jackie Robinson broke baseball's color line—there was only an abiding sense of patriotism and personal growth. In my purview, it was the start of a brand new life, a whole new way of living. The olive brown of the uniform may have been called military drabs, or fatigues, but to me the uniform was like a bright palette. The first thing I learned to do was an "about-face" because it looked so soldierly, crisply turning on a dime with a shift on my feet. And the order arms drill? Forget it. To perfect that move was to reach the gate of nirvana. My faculties and concentration focused for the first time, I sailed through basic training, and my exuberance and eagerness to obey orders must have made me seem rather unique.

In what seemed like the blink of an eye, this teenage dropout from Central Avenue was now on his way to Japan with the 24th Infantry -- and he would be soldiering under General Douglas MacArthur's occupation forces of vanquished Japan. This was still a year before the order came down to integrate the armed forces, and no black soldiers were stationed in Tokyo.

Instead, we were kept in the shadows, in Gifu, a city of 180,000 people in central Japan that has since become famous for its fashion district and the Nawa Insect Museum. It was a bustling river city, and during the war its factories had turned out fire balloons—hot air balloons turned into airborne bombs—and sent them riding the jet stream of the Pacific en route to the west coast of America; undetected by radar, the range of these balloons was much greater than that of bomber planes that needed to refuel along the way. A few of the fire balloons made it to the US, though the only fatalities occurred after the war when an Oregon church group came upon an unexploded one, and accidently detonated it, resulting in the deaths of five children and one adult.

According to the official picture of Gifu painted by the U.S. government and the Army, the Japanese welcomed us as if they loved us; they lavished us with affection, as friends -- and even threw us parades. This all stemmed from the fact that MacArthur was a hero, damn near a deity, to the Japanese. And that was true, at least in Tokyo among those politicians who wanted to curry his favor in order to further themselves in a post-war government. In fact, if there was one word, I would choose to describe the Japanese, it was cunning. That was the trait that created their imperialism, using the element of surprise to occupy all those islands in the South Pacific and, of course, their sneak attack on Pearl Harbor. Once the element of surprise was gone and America had driven them back to their homeland, that was all she wrote.

But the Japanese maintained their cunning in cozying up to MacArthur, and when they were handed the reins to their government, we know how they continued a different sort of imperialism—economic imperialism—by infiltrating markets around the world, borrowing from their technologies, and creating cheaper products that would undercut those markets. During the 1970s, we here in America witnessed a peacetime invasion, when Japan moved on to new heights in dominating the electronics and automobile markets.

Incidentally, the Japanese didn't encourage black businessmen to own dealerships, but one must give the Japanese credit for their post-war economic ingenuity. The country has been a loyal ally of ours, however I cannot vouch for any attempts by the government or the people to accept what was a very humanitarian occupation by the country they had attacked on a quiet Sunday morning only a few years earlier. We had no agenda to punish them, yet they showed the same disrespect for the black soldiers as the rednecks at home did. They even went out their way to prevent us from visiting their prostitutes.

That sounds like a flippant remark, but it's a hundred percent accurate. Gifu had a bustling red-light district where the ladies of the night serviced the Japanese merchant marines whose ships docked on the nearby Kiso River. But because the natives so hated—or feared—the black soldiers, women were actually transferred to Tokyo, which was off-limits to us. I found it remarkable that they would go to such lengths to keep a black man from touching a Japanese woman. That's not to say that black men didn't find their way to the women. I knew some who not only found them and entered into relationships but would go on to marry them and bring them home to America as war brides.

Instead of searching out female companionship, my priority was improving myself. I spent almost three years in Japan, using my time to get an education. I learned to speak a little bit of Japanese. I enrolled in the Army Education Program in Yokohama, Hiyoshi, and Keio, earning certificates in criminology, welding, and carpentry. I even got my picture into some papers back home when the Army gathered some of us in the program for a public relations photo. I was tested for military aptitude by the Armed Forces Institute in Tokyo and finished in the top 15th or 20th percentiles in correctness and effectiveness of expression, interpretation of social studies, natural sciences, literacy materials, and mathematical ability. I believed— foolishly, it turned out—that this would only help usher me toward a commission as an officer in the U.S. military.

In sum, I was of two minds about Japan. I loved how industrious and imaginative they were, but the people had no affection for black Americans, and the prejudice I developed was, admittedly, not something I was proud of.

My hitch was over in the summer of 1950, and I returned home, no longer an aimless seventeen-year-old kid, but as a twenty-year-old man. I had begun to mull over what I would do with myself. I wanted to remain in uniform either as a firefighter or policeman. This was wishful thinking, to be sure, as there were no blacks employed in the Hackensack Fire Department—save for a man named Arthur Rochester—and almost none in the police department. However, the drums of another war were already in the air. Few in America seemed to be aware of the conflict in Korea. That scarred country, liberated from Japanese control, had been divided into two zones at the 38th Parallel, with Russia and China controlling the north, and the U.S. (technically under the new banner of the United Nations), the south. In 1948, these zones had become North and South Korea, the former ruled by Kim Il-Sung, the grandfather of the pudgy little fellow we've seen too much of the last few years, Kim Jong-un. South Korea was ruled by Syngman Rhee, another authoritarian. But he was our authoritarian.

In June 1950, after years of skirmishes, North Korean tanks rolled across the border and overwhelmed the ill-equipped South Korean army. President Truman responded by sending in U.S. forces, tapping MacArthur to be the U.N.'s commanding general. By then, Truman's edict to integrate the military had gone into effect, if uneasily. My pulse quickened at the thought of putting my skills to good use in a war. I was thirsty for action, for combat. I had not used a gun in anything but controlled training situations. Now I would be doing what I was trained to do.

I had inquired about re-upping and transferring to Korea prior to being sent back to the US, but my discharge papers had already been issued, and so I was put on a transport ship, the USS *James O'Hara*, for the journey homeward. Just my luck—the day after, Truman would freeze all discharges and furloughs. Although many men not eager to face bullets in battle would not have cursed that as bad fortune, but I was frustrated. When I got home to New Jersey, I enjoyed a brief time with my family. My mother was pleased to know I had become not only a man but a disciplined soldier. I was assigned to Fort Dix once more; the war having made it necessary for even discharged soldiers to re-take training in the event more troops would be needed. Once there, I would re-enlist.

With fellow soldiers in Korea

With fellow soldiers in Korea

As an MP in Japan

My trusty sidearm

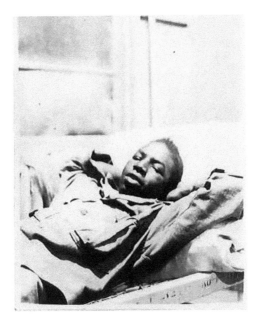

Catching some down-time in Japan

CHAPTER 2

A WAR TO FIGHT

When I returned to Fort Dix, integration had been mandated, but there were worries among the black GIs. First Sergeant Harry L. Myles thought he should speak up about it. "Gentlemen," he said to the troops, as we stood erect in an early-morning reveille formation, "integration is not going to alter our behavior. We coloreds will soldier as we have never soldiered before." The only problem was, the Army threw a monkey wrench into my plans, all but labeling me a criminal on the most specious of grounds. The only positive thing about the experience was that it heightened my awareness that, in matters of race, the military had not changed all that much since the men of the Deuce-Four— "mockingbirds," as they were derisively dubbed by Army prosecutors—were thrown to the wolves thirty years before.

Just by way of context, let the record show that the majority of court-martials were for mostly minor offenses—which, not coincidentally, was a means by which racism could fester, since black soldiers were inordinately accused of such offenses. Even a man of high character and honor like Jackie Robinson was court-martialed for the crime of being black. The essence of the charge brought against him in 1944 at Fort Hood, Texas, was that he refused to ride in the back of a bus. This, too, had the stench of the mockingbirds, though, happily, Jackie was quickly acquitted. In other words, military justice, as it applied to black men, was a game played by small men with small minds who had been born of privilege; they sought to keep a lid on integration and, to them, the Truman order was merely a piece of paper. In the real world, Southern whites still called the shots, and they had no reason to alter their natural proclivities. Let the record also show that I was, in the strictest sense, guilty—and should have been applauded for it.

Here's how the story goes: It began with a training exercise in late October that lasted an entire day. The men returned in full gear, exhausted, half past dead. Basic training is not a picnic in the country, its rules could have been written by the Marquis de Sade. The same men would need to get up at 4:00 a.m. the next day and do it all over again. I was on guard duty that night at the pump station in New Lisbon, New Jersey and I decided to let the trainees doze an hour longer. I did not wake them for reveille. I thought little of it; the military code is strict, but a little empathy and common sense go hand-in-hand with discipline. I'm sure the men appreciated getting that extra hour of sleep and were sharper that day for it. It didn't seem like a big deal at the time. My next-in-command didn't say anything about it. A few days later I did the same thing again. But someone must have snitched to the brass, and when they saw that the sentry hadn't gone by the book—and was a young black man—the wheels of military justice began to roll, right over me.

On November 18, 1950, I was arraigned on two articles of misconduct for violating the 86th Article of War. The charge was that I "was found sleeping on post." This was news to me. I absolutely did not fall asleep on duty. I took the fall for not waking my fellow soldiers for reveille, and I had no compunction saying it was a noble thing to do. Those men needed rest. I pleaded not guilty and testified before the motley crew of officers deciding the case. "These guys worked hard," I said. "I let them get some more rest." I don't recall whether the Army even had a witness testify against me; it was all pro forma. They had a chance to brand a black man. Even so, I could tell these white judges were somewhat surprised that I—or that any black man could have—defended myself. I articulately and passionately explained that I had bent the rules for the benefit of exhausted soldiers in training. I was, for all to see, a good soldier. That they could not deny.

On December 1, the court ruled: guilty on the main charge, not guilty on what was called an "Additional Charge," whatever that was. The sentence was that I would be "reduced to the lowest enlisted grade"—which was exactly what I was at the time anyway— "be confined at hard labor" for three months and be fined $31 for each of those three months. For a PFC, ninety-three bucks was a pretty fair portion of his income. As it played out, however, by the following July, an appeals court said, in effect, never mind. They handed down a ruling setting aside the guilty verdict and returning the money that had been withheld from my pay, saying only, "All rights, privileges, and property of which the accused has been deprived . . . will be restored."

Fortunately, this judicial charade did not cause me to lose my good name. No one at Fort Dix took the court-martial seriously, least of all me. Even so, this kerfuffle slowed my path to Korea. It would take another year before I could get off the base where I should have spent just a few months. That ate at me. The silver lining was that all the time I spent on this trivial prosecution put me into a kind of classroom, absorbing the grinding process of a court-martial: the process, the jargon, the documents, the testimony, the wide latitude of the officers sitting in judgment, even what I perceived to be their inner thoughts and conflicts. All of these lessons would later go into the writing of my book *Farewell to the Mockingbirds*. So, I thank the lords of the military court for enlightening me, even as they tarred me.

The Army wanted me to be in the Engineer Corps, but I was adamant. "I want Infantry," I said. "And I want to be on the front lines. The. Front. Lines." They could see my sincerity, my intensity. So, headquarters changed the orders that had already been drawn up for my reenlistment...and I was reassigned to Company K, 9th Infantry Regiment, 2nd Infantry Division.

The 9th had been an all-black unit before President Truman, in July 1948, issued the historic Executive Order 9981 abolishing discrimination in the Armed Forces (as well as in the entirety of the U.S. government). Implementing the order, however, was a drawn-out process that took four years. In the transition, black units were converted to mostly white. I was never comfortable in that setting, but somehow, we did manage to dodge the vitriol one would expect from the integration of the races. It was not as embittered as we anticipated it would be. There were few out-and-out fights, but racism simmered below the surface and reared its head in more subtle ways.

It was under these uncertain circumstances that I would meet a fellow New Jerseyan, Al Freed, who was very quick to tell you that he was Jewish. Al was one of the men with whom I was assigned to the 9th when we shipped out to Korea. He later wrote:

"James and I had a bond. He's from Hackensack; I'm from Passaic. We were the only non-Southern boys in the 9th after they reorganized it for integration. It had been an all-black outfit—the white soldiers called it the Bugout 9th because the rednecks liked to say that black soldiers would retreat under fire—but now it was almost all white, and the whites were rednecks. Jim was about the only black guy, and I think I was the only Jew. But he became popular. Wonderful guy, bright, funny, well read. He could put into words what we couldn't. When guys wanted to write letters to their wives or girlfriends back home, they had Jim do it for them because he could sweet-talk the ladies, or he could make them cry. He probably saved a lot of guys' marriages from cracking up. Many years later, I saw him on the Johnny Carson Show, and he was the same guy. He didn't change a bit. Let me tell you, he was good to have on your side. I weighed about 140 pounds soaking wet and he was big and strong, around 180. Nobody messed with me when he was around."

Actually, there were three other black soldiers with me in the battalion, and any problems with assimilation were smothered over by our collective pride. We were a hell of a fighting unit. We were cocky. And I would become more so.

In the late summer of 1952, I was finally stationed in South Korea. It was a contingent of about two hundred men stationed in the steamy Kumwha Valley, an arid, mountainous region close to the border of North Korea. By now, MacArthur was gone. The old warhorse, inured to being swathed in honor and glory, could not adapt to the new realities of war. His vanity could not reconcile what he saw as clear solutions to thorny problems. With the Russians threatening to ally with the Chinese, and the costly advance-and-retreat nature of this war, he wanted to drop a nuke or two, not only on enemy installations, but on sites within the USSR. That might have sparked World War III, but his feeling was that if such a holocaust were inevitable, now was the time to get the drop on the Russians, who were gobbling up Eastern Europe behind the Iron Curtain. When Truman rebuffed him, MacArthur, a Caesar-like figure, tried to leverage his enormous popularity to overrule the president. It didn't work. Instead, MacArthur was relieved of his duty on April 10, 1951, his command taken over by General Matthew Ridgeway. Although I had not the slightest say in strategies or geopolitical factors, it was obvious to me that our objectives in this fight were hazy, compromised by a strategy of containment rather than unambiguous victory. Regardless, I was expecting to serve for a good long while in Korea.

The first time I tasted combat, shoulder to shoulder with white soldiers, I saw an enemy soldier in the distance walking along a ridgeline behind some barbed wire. At the time, the war had become a two-year stalemate. The wild card was China, which was providing military support for the Communist North Koreans. Chinese troops had come across the border in 1950, but our forces had pushed them back to the famous 38th parallel. Still, we could see that the Chinese were constantly crossing into Southern territory, a clear violation of the tenuous peace agreement in effect and killing our guys with seeming impunity. From my perch, I bore witness to the emergence of China as an enemy that would not recede.

As it happened, it was a fully uniformed Chinese soldier who I had to beat one-on-one. While on my very first patrol, the Chinese on our turf had learned we were in the area and began banging tin cans, which was their signal to man their guns. When this soldier walked out of his bunker from right to left, the light of the moon hit him exactly right.

Boom.

I fired once. He was gone. A perfect kill shot.

I'll never forget the moment he fell. And let me correct myself here. He didn't fall; he crumpled down to the ground—he did it like a shadow that had nothing left to cling to. He was no more than a silhouette to me that night, but later I began to wonder: Was the outlined figure married? Did he have a son? A daughter? A family? Did the silhouette have anybody who cared? That was my first taste of war. It was bitter, but in a battle of kill or be killed, I was the one who walked away.

Only days later I would have my second taste of combat and this time it was my own choice.

To re-live means to go back—back, to that one particularly hot August night in the hills of Korea. On August 15, a fiery lieutenant named Henry Schenk, our erstwhile platoon leader, called the company together. He was the prototypical officer and a gentleman. Having been born in Austria, he spoke German fluently and had been an interpreter for the prosecutors at the Nazi war trials in Nuremberg. With jet-black hair slicked back, he was dashing; he had a movie-star allure. He announced he was looking for volunteers to go behind enemy lines. An American soldier had been taken prisoner by the Communists, stripped naked, and hung upside down on a barren tree on the side of a hill as a warning to our troops. The area had been bombarded into a wasteland, and the prisoner in question was about twelve miles away. We would need to go on foot, step by step, through the pitch darkness.

There were thousands of North Koreans and their Chinese allies out there just across the border, and probably quite a few on our side as well. Our forces had already captured approximately 40,000 prisoners. We knew they greatly outnumbered us. We would have to be small and mobile to proceed unnoticed. The plan was to rescue our guy, then get the hell out before the enemy was any the wiser. To call it dangerous would be a gross understatement, but I didn't hesitate. There were a small number of us who volunteered, signing on to a mission that probably had no better than a ten percent chance of succeeding. If it failed, no one was likely to make it back. Some of the guys called it a suicide mission. Al thought I was crazy. He later said:

"I didn't go on that patrol because it was doomed to fail. When you go out into enemy territory, you need firepower as backup. They had just their own weapons. Jim McEachin had a Thompson submachine gun. I don't know where he got it, because it wasn't a standard issue weapon. He said before he left, "With this thing, I can hold off a whole regiment!" But most of them never got to use what they had. That's how sudden the end came."

What it boiled down to was that Lieutenant Schenk was in on it, so I wanted in, too. And he must have liked my spunk because he chose me as the point man, the leader of the mission—or the proverbial sacrificial lamb, for I would be the first soldier the enemy would see.

We waited for the cover of darkness. It was a brutally hot night, and we had to pack our gear and weapons. We carried our M1 rifles, .45 sidearms, and ammo belts. We were weighted down with all this hardware, and in the humid air our brows were sweating under our helmets, our feet burning in our heavy boots.

It was about to get a lot hotter. We didn't know it, but we had walked right smack into an ambush, the captured American soldier being the lure. After hours of slowly trudging forward in silence, in the blink of an eye the sky lit up like the Fourth of July and smoke was everywhere. I would later write of that moment of terror:

"There's so much fire from rifles, machine guns, bazookas, carbines, grenade launchers, and sidearms that we can almost taste the gunpowder. Schenk is a fighting machine. But he is also in shock. The Chinese rake his area with fire, but Schenk refuses to go down, the muzzle of his weapon spitting fire, on his knees, cursing, shouting, firing. An explosion hits him; two more men go down, one screaming for his mother."

I say with all sincerity and sadness that Lt. Henry Schenk was the bravest man I ever knew. But I saw him pay the ultimate price. His gun went silent, and he crumpled to the ground. He was cut to pieces by bullets. I knew he was dead.

Meanwhile, those of us who were still alive were scrambling for our lives, looking to take cover in the underbrush, but they had booby-trapped the woods, and all I heard was guys crying out in pain. All I could see was the flash of gunfire as I was engulfed by thick, billowing smoke. We couldn't even set ourselves to fire our weapons. We were just scrambling in chaos. I didn't know how many of us had gone down. I felt a bullet pierce my thigh, then, in the next split-second, an explosion literally lifted me off my feet, and everything went dark.

The hills felt like they were still on fire when I regained consciousness. I remember the struggle of getting to my knees, trying to breathe deeply, and cupping my hand to form a ladle so that I could swallow sips of water to quench the fire below. My stomach, a portion of which was being held in with a free hand, was bleeding badly. I had never felt so much pain. I was sweating, fighting mosquitoes, and recoiling at the thought of drinking more of the water pooled around lumpy, iridescent-looking rocks that lay at the edge of the creek. Something told me then, hang tight. Better days are coming. I thought of my Grandmother Becky.

It's all a matter of attitude, thus I've made attitude a practice. I have been hanging tight ever since that awful moment. Decades, in fact, I eventually learned from aging and from a tired, old, scarred-up body that one does not completely heal from war—nor, for that matter, from being that close to death. But at all costs, no matter the adversity, something has always said to me, Hang tight. Psychologically, war-time scars never heal. More than once I could have or should have died, and in a figurative sense, maybe I did. Maybe I died in little pieces—or you might say, in the little pieces of me that were scattered on that Korean front.

Let it be said I survived the ordeal because of a savior above and a savior below, a soldier who I did not know and whose name I never would know. Only I and one other soldier on the patrol survived the ambush. I've asked myself—too often for my own good, I suppose— why me, why not them? Was I a better Christian? Did it matter? Did anything matter? Does anything matter? Beating or cheating death leaves one with a greater appreciation of life. The air does smell fresher, food does taste better, the sky does look bluer. But fear is fixed; the salve of survival can't fully bathe those scars away. They hurt, forever, forcing you to adapt but never heal. The mind can't be locked against the intrusion of sudden, dead-of- night resurrections of terror and fear. Survival sometimes can be worse than the alternative unless you can set yourself free from the burden of memory.

Troop Ship

CHAPTER 3

A JESUS FIGURE

I didn't move for what seemed like hours, bleeding from leg and stomach wounds, lying in a shallow, polluted creek. I awoke in the dim light of dawn, the sky a sheet of fog, the landscape silent emptiness. I felt jagged metal sticking out of my midsection and leg, and I could feel and hear the drip, drip, drip of blood. Under normal circumstances, I would have bled to death, my life slowly oozing into that awful creek. My face was so close to the dirty, polluted water that I inhaled some of it, doing permanent damage to my lungs and causing me to later develop pleurisy, an inflammation of the lungs that makes breathing a real struggle. I can still taste that grotesque swill, still feel the burn in my throat.

There was little I could do except lay there and wait, hoping for rescue but anticipating death. And then, in the stillness, a voice. When I first heard it, I couldn't tell if it was friend or foe. Then the hushed voice rang out again – more muffled, but it worked: "Halt! Who goes?"

Hearing English was reassuring, to put it mildly. I could see through squinting eyes that he was a soldier. His face was angular; blond hair jutted from under his helmet. Aided by the luminous light of a low hanging moon, he seemed to be Germanic or Scandinavian, though he spoke with no discernible regional accent. As he neared, his gun remained drawn and pointed, until he saw by the color of my skin and tattered fatigues that I, too, was an American.

Kneeling beside me, he said, almost laconically, "What are you doing here?"

In semi-coherence, I challenged him and then went on to explain about the patrol and the ambush. At that point, I didn't know only two of us had survived. I knew bodies were strewn out there. I didn't know how many because I couldn't remember had been on the patrol in the first place. I figured this mystery soldier had to know something more of the ambush, but he said nothing. He tried lifting me to the embankment, but my pain prevented it. As time went on, he tried to lift me with different positions, different body angles and with various hand placements, under my armpits, around my chest, but to no avail.

In the distance, I could hear faint voices speaking in what I figured out to be Chinese. They were either advancing or withdrawing, I don't know. If the former, there was only a brief period of time to get out or be taken prisoner—a fate we knew could be worse than death. Given what we heard they did to POWs, and particularly the wounded, I'd rather have the maggots feast on my body than be tortured and starved to death. After all, we had gone on this mission because one of our troops had been killed and left naked and hanging upside down from a tree.

I remembered the vow I had made to myself even during basic training back at Fort Dix. I said I would never be taken prisoner, particularly if I had been wounded. And no doubt I had been wounded in four different places -- to include the liver and spleen, as I was later to find out.

The enigmatic soldier tried his damnedest to remove me from the creek. Finally, slipping and sliding, he was able to get me out of the water. When it was safe, he applied a tourniquet to my thigh and a pressure bandage to my stomach wound. Throughout the procedure, he was quiet and comforting. He was focused, energetic, and knowledgeable, He had spring in his step. But then, later that day, after he had carried me for yet another long walk, he sat me down and propped me up under a tree, suddenly, he began to walk away. Stroking his chin, looking all around. Now, backing away. In my semi-delirium, my mind jumped to one possible conclusion. I didn't want to think this way, but was he ...abandoning me, leaving me to die in enemy territory? Had he given up on carrying me out and was now saying to me to hell with it? Was an American soldier going to let a brother-in-arms die?

War has no rules, no etiquette, no assumption of humanity or morality. Not all battles end in bravery: some end in cowardice. Something inside of me snapped. As dazed as I was, I felt a cold chill run down my spine. My eyes narrowed. I still had my .45, and before he got too far away, maybe another 10 or 15 yards and I would reach for it. If I was going down, I would not be going down alone: The soldier who gave up on me would go down with me. I'm not proud of what I was thinking, but in that sequence, when humanity and conscience didn't exist, and with a soldier's blind justice taking place of tender mercy, I had my orders, coming from a place within me I didn't know existed.

Fortunately for both of us, perhaps a second or two before the synapse from my brain jumped into my index finger, he turned and came back to where I lay, clutching my stomach with one hand and trying to tend to my thigh with the other. It became clear to me that all the young blond boy wanted to do was to do was to survey the lay of the land for the best route back to our line without fear of mines or the Chinese we had heard earlier. In hindsight, that split-second is the precise moment when my better angels held off my suicide—as I surely would have put the next bullet after killing him into my own skull, a murder-suicide on the battlefield.

I have asked myself night after night -- if the roles had been reversed and I had come upon this "brother" in arms. half-submerged in that water, whether I would have done all that he did for me, to save him? And though it sounds bathetic, my answer has always been, and will always be, that the goodness and kindness in my heart will always outweigh any and all other traits and that the better angels will prevail.

I can justify ambivalence by noting the inviolate truism that "War is hell," the wisest and most profound sentence ever uttered by mankind. Unless you have been in war, or under the gun and in the shadow of death reigning down from the sky, you cannot ever fathom the push and pull of conflicting emotions. What that soldier did required more than bravery; it required great strength and a flash of insanity. I may have had the insanity. I don't know if I had that kind of inner strength or courage.

Moral conundrums aside, the soldier never knew how close he came to being left for the buzzard. Now he still faced the stupefying task of getting us safely back to our lines. He had me slung me over his back, my legs dangling like strands of a mop. I was completely in his hands.

Whether to sit me down or keep moving, it was his decision. I didn't even know if we were headed in the right direction. Shells were lobbed at us from afar, and I could hear Chinese voices out there somewhere.

We just kept moving on, relentlessly. Several times during the piggy-back ride, crazy with thirst, I blacked out, coming to for only a few moments at a time.

During one moment of lucidity, I asked his name. He smiled thinly and politely declined. "I think it's better to keep it that way," he said softly. "Names have a way of changing things; people, places—maybe even races. This way we can always remember ourselves as being ourselves— brothers under the skin. It's called being a brother to a brother."

Somehow, I managed to smile back. "I like that," I said. "I like it a lot."

To my everlasting regret, even anger, I retain no memory of when or how the soldier dropped me at the camp. I can only recall that one of the soldiers called as I was brought in, "Oh God, look at him!" In time, I learned that only two men had survived the patrol, which I assumed were me and the blond-haired soldier. But I never did find out if he was the second, or whether he was in our company or not. He just seemed to vanish.

The doctors disinfected and bandaged the wounds. I was put on a gurney, loaded onto something like a trolley tram, flown by helicopter to an airfield, then taken by plane to Yokohama, Japan for proper treatment at a hospital. They fixed me up to their satisfaction. Most of the wounds were superficial and no bones were broken. All in all, I was pretty lucky. Damned lucky. The doctors said to me: "You'll be running soon. You're doing great. You've got it made."

But their optimism was belied by intense pain. I could barely stand erect. Gunpowder and shrapnel fragments were left in my gut and leg, and the metal stitches they sewed me up with were thick and troublesome. I feared I would be permanently bent over, and though I eventually could straighten up, the wounds would disfigure me. The shrapnel would feel as if they were bursting through my skin. The pain would be chronic. To make things worse, the place itself was getting to be a bother. It was getting so I couldn't take it anymore. I couldn't keep abreast of the news about the war because someone in the hospital stole my radio. They also took my girlfriend's picture. The bastards!

In the aftermath of the ambush, a search and rescue team from regimental headquarters was sent to recover the remains of the dead. No bodies were found, leading to speculation that the enemy had taken them. The only personal item found was a combat boot with an embedded serial number— that of Lt. Henry A. Schenk. Moreover, there seemed to be confusion about my rescue. As Al Freed recalls it:

"What happened was, they walked into an ambush. And I was his buddy, so I went out on the patrol to look for him. It was mid-day. We sent up some smoke flares so he could know we were coming for him. Someone saw him through binoculars in a rice paddy. He had three bullets in his stomach. He was unconscious and we brought him back. I don't know about a blond soldier, but other units also had gone out to find him. All I know is we found him in that rice paddy, and I was so relieved Jim was alive."

In many ways, my rescue is a mystery. I don't recall ever having been in a rice paddy. Conceivably, the blond-haired boy could have handed me off to our guys. We were originally told that a second soldier had survived the ambush, yet no other man was ever identified as the other survivor. Make of it what you like, but there is no mystery for me in that contradiction. The second survivor was the one who found me.

I have tried many times through the years to track him down with no luck. Often, I would pass by a man with blond hair and other seemingly telling features and wonder, "Is that him?" Over time, I had to let go of trying to find my rescuer. I had my life to live, I needed to put distance between that ambush and the present, and I needed to wean myself from the military mindset.

The epilogue of that night and morning in hell is that I saw a Jesus figure in that blond-haired boy, emerging out of the smoky haze of bullets and bombs. In every way, it was biblical, and while I am not a religious fanatic, nor do I believe in idolatry, I cannot see it any other way. The soldier with no name was more than a mere mortal. He was a savior. I sometimes say that had I pulled the trigger on him, I would have shot the son of God. It sounds insane, but then, what is war if not the height of insanity?

War can change a man in a split-second, before his eyes can see or his mind can think. It can burrow so deeply into the mind that the most traumatic of events are stripped from conscious memory. That is the only rational explanation I can provide for why I have no clear recollection of how that blond savior got me back to my base. Most of it was blacked out—gone—as was what happened after the docs treated me.

As best I can piece it together in the years since, I walked out of the hospital, wearing civilian clothes that had been provided to me there. Technically, that meant I was AWOL, and I only wish I could tell you whether that diversion was worth it, for I have no idea what I did in Yokohama or wherever I was. I am sure it would be quite an intriguing story. In the bigger picture, which would become clearer to me in the future, did the military keep me active because I was a black man seemingly programmed to fight? I have gone through life with pieces of shrapnel in my leg and gut, pieces that show up on every X-ray I've had taken. Doctors tell me there are fragments of bullet stuck between my ribs. And I wonder why those pieces are there. Could the doctors in Tokyo have left them there so they could move me out quickly?

Word had gotten around of my rescue from certain death. My mother and siblings were shocked and frightened when they received a telegram signed by General William E. Bergin on August 21, a week after the ambush, informing them with "deep regret that your son PFC McEachin, James E., Jr. was wounded in action in Korea." A second telegram to them starkly revealed the extent of my injuries, saying that "the wounds were of a serious nature consisting of shell fragments penetrating the abdomen and right thigh, with other wounds of the liver."

I was awarded the Silver Star—though I did not actually receive the medal and would not for decades. On September 2, 1952, New Jersey U. S. Senator, Robert Hendrickson wrote to me on Senate letterhead:

"My Dear Private McEachin,

I have just learned from the Department of Defense of the heroic contribution you have made in foreign fields, that liberty and justice may continue in this great land of ours.

As a veteran of two wars, I know something of the pain and suffering, not to mention the anguish, which accompany battle wounds. I sincerely trust that the injury you have sustained will heal with all due speed. In the meanwhile, you have my deepest sympathy, as well as my profound gratitude for the service you have rendered for your country and for all of us who are privileged to live within its borders."

A month later, the Army gave me another stripe, promoting me to corporal. It was a change that meant little, as a corporal was actually just a glorified private, but I wore that extra stripe on my sleeve with pride when, again rather than sending me home, my order was to go back to Korea. I can recall no explanation of why, nor can I recall arriving at Company K, 2nd Infantry encampment, which had moved to Koje Island.

I shook my head in wonder when Al Freed later told of seeing me suddenly pop up out of the past:

"One day a white car drove onto our grounds. I looked closer and saw none other than Jim at the wheel. I had last seen him on a stretcher being sent to a hospital. But now, there he was, smiling and waving at everybody. We just stood there, dumbfounded, rubbing our eyes in disbelief. You never even saw officers driving a flashy car. I never knew they even had cars over there, just those jeeps. We weren't in a big, secure base in Japan or even Seoul. This was in the middle of nowhere. So how the hell did Jim get to arrive in a white car? Again, as I say, Jim was born to steal scenes."

I ask that question, as well: How the hell did I arrive in a white car? Like Al, I break out in laughter about this Hollywood-style entrance, right out of *M*A*S*H*, and damn, I wish I could remember how it happened. I have mulled over various scenarios trying to fill the voids in memory. Could I have somehow talked my way into being sent back to Korea, and agreed to drive an officer's car from an air base to the camp? Was it all kept on the downlow because officers weren't supposed to have private cars? Had I demanded to be returned to the war instead of going home? Did they just stitch me up and put a rifle back in my hands, thinking I would be eager to volunteer for another suicide mission? I have often wondered about this and have invited possible explanations from anyone who has a theory.

The hardest question about my tour in Korea is this: Why did my mind block out so much? It is a conundrum I'm forced to live with. I'm convinced that I had a severe case of post-traumatic stress disorder, my psychological damage no less severe than the physical injuries that had almost killed me. This self-diagnosis would be corroborated through the years by mental health professionals who I have confided in: My subconscious immediately erected barriers to insulate me from reliving my near-death experience. I had seen Lt. Schenk killed in a hail of bullets before I was hit, but there may well have been other horrific things I saw while drifting in and out of consciousness, images that would haunt me forever if I had to live with those sights and sounds.

Again, there is an ironic postscript in that I have been haunted anyway. And perhaps writing about being haunted has somehow helped me make peace with the subconscious demons. Yet, even at my age, the mental shadows linger, most vividly in the darkness of night. That is the most enduring souvenir of war for me. The only one now, really, since the pearl-handled .45 I carried into battle was stolen from my home several years ago. I can live without the .45. It's much harder to live with the demons. That is my world without end.

I grapple with the holes in my memory frequently and I would pursue answers for decades. My 201 records—or military personnel file—were misplaced, or so I was told. It was also said that some of my records were destroyed by the big fire that occurred in St. Louis some years ago, and that I could only rely on the personal reminiscences of men like Al Freed. Other than Freed, the closest I came to finding some substantiating truth about my memories was one who had served and been friends with Lt. Schenk, a man by the name of Colonel Joseph Ferko, Jr. When I was able to track him down, I was on cloud nine. When we spoke on the phone, I told him that I thought Lt. Schenk deserved the Medal of Honor, and Ferko, now retired, agreed. We planned to collaborate on writing up the commendation. However, Ferko died only days before we had arranged to meet. It was a definite setback, because he had served with Schenk and had kept Schenk's morning reports as souvenirs. When Ferko passed, so did my opportunity to answer the questions that had needled me for years.

All through the years since Korea, my injuries have taunted me; there is no escaping them. Only after the war did I learn of the damage to my lungs caused by that fetid pool of water I landed in after the grenade knocked me off my feet. I developed pleurisy and tuberculosis, and other maladies, leading to the removal of part of a lung and lung cancer - neither of which slowed me down a bit. For me, though, more painful than my physical ailments is the reaction some have had to my story of survival. Recently, during a routine medical appointment at the VA hospital, a doctor asked me, "Mr. McEachin, have you had any brain injuries?" I took that to mean, as others had inferred, that he thought I was given to hallucinations because of my repeated visits to the clinic. I assured him that my brain was intact and was responsible for my ability to memorize scripts and write multiple books. What he didn't seem to understand was that the injury was to my subconscious, hidden in a dungeon for which I cannot find a key.

The war I came back to had become a stalemate. Guys were dying for nothing but pride and face-saving. Generals came and went like the change of seasons. At least two were even taken prisoner. The first one, General William F. Dean, who had led American forces in Burma in World War II, took over command of the 24th Infantry. A proactive type, Dean went into battle himself, firing away at North Korean tanks and disabling one, whereupon he told the press, "I just got me a Red tank!" But Dean became stranded and was captured and sent to a POW camp. Held for three years, he was tortured but never cracked. Given the Medal of Honor while missing in action, he was released in 1953 and said, "I'm no hero. Anybody dumb enough to get captured doesn't deserve to be a hero."

Dumb, indeed, was the second general. I should know. We had been assigned to guard the enemy prisoners who were being held in seventeen installations on Koje Island. There were around 40,000 of them in seven compounds, and if it sounds like this was tailor-made for chaos, it was.

Unlike the Koreans and Chinese, we abided by the Geneva Convention— perhaps too willingly. We bent over backwards to accommodate prisoners, many of whom were smarter than our own officers, persuading them to permit all sorts of concessions, one of which was that the prisoners could make North Korean flags to wave, the red in the flag created by their own blood. It was impossible to watch out for everything going on in those compounds.

Some were in cities and there would be women who came right up to the fence wearing baskets on their heads—the signal that they were, let's say, readily available, and it could happen right through the fence! When we got wise to that, we used those women to spy on the prisoners for us. Because there was an army within an army in there; some were officers, and the enemy would sneak information in to them to try to set up an escape. So, we would send the women over there to strike up a conversation, and they would return and tell us if there was something going on that we should know about. Some would play both sides; they would be paid by the Communists to deliver information; then be paid by us to say what the information was. They were the best-looking double agents there could be.

The situation was almost like *Hogan's Heroes*, except it wasn't funny. Due to the lax conditions, an American battalion was attacked in a horrendous security breach, the inmates killing one American soldier while over a hundred POWs were wounded. The camps were so overcrowded that they spilled over to some South Korean cities. We just couldn't control the mass of humanity behind those gates. In February 1952, General Francis Dodd, the chief of staff for Eighth Army General James Van Fleet, came to inspect the compounds under his watch. He was listening to complaints by prisoners, why I don't know, when a gate was opened for a brief moment, and he was snared and taken hostage. Try to picture that—an American general was taken hostage by prisoners of his own POW camp!

I don't know if that has ever happened in the history of the United States military, and teeth-gnashing embarrassment at Army headquarters in Seoul and Washington, D.C., must have set off a tempest. Dodd was held for seventy-eight hours as negotiations went on between the prisoners and our command—again, try to picture that happening in our own POW camp. It also led me to question my own actions. The harmless fun I'd had tricking the Chinese prisoners into thinking I was speaking to them in their language may have gotten a rise out of our guys, but it could have been taken by the enemy officers as a sign of the Americans' permissiveness.

In any case, rather than having us go in with guns blazing to rescue him, another general, Charles Colson, was sent in with orders to make a fictitious admission that we had mistreated the prisoners—an enormous propaganda victory for them. Dodd was rightly savaged in the press, busted down to colonel, and forced to retire (his rank would be restored in the 1970s after he died). Colson was reassigned, also branded in infamy. The next man on the griddle, General Hayden Boatner—the fourteenth commander of the camps in sixteen months—promised to be tougher, but the die was cast. A lot of people in high places didn't have a clue as to how to run a war. The enemy knew that if they hung on, public opinion against the war in America would lead us to pull up stakes. And as if this wasn't self-defeating enough, the racism that Truman's order intended to at least mitigate was a continuing source of discontent among the black soldiers.

As I learned firsthand by my ludicrous court-martial, black soldiers were brought up on bogus charges of misconduct at a much higher rate than were the white soldiers. They were given menial tasks and kept from promotion. Most of the officers seemed to be white Southern men, promoted by rote, which dashed my long-held dream of being commissioned. Not even serving with valor in combat swayed minds in the upper echelon of the military to promote some of the finest soldiers we had. I can say without reservation that most of the white soldiers I served with, including officers, had but a fraction of the dedication and sobriety of their black counterparts—because the latter had to be better, to prove they weren't inferior. True, I had not personally encountered that much static. Perhaps I could just ignore it better. For those who could not, repeated calls of "nigger" or "coon" were like stinging slaps to the face. And it came from everyone from privates to high officers.

I recently was sent a quite fascinating memoir by Curtis James Morrow, a fellow black Korean War vet, provocatively titled *What's a Commie Ever Done to Black People? A Korean War Memoir of Fighting in the U.S. Army's Last All Negro Unit* (channeling Muhammad Ali's famous phrase during the Vietnam war, "I ain't got no quarrel with them Viet Cong"). Like me, Curtis enlisted at age seventeen and served in the 24th Infantry. He later wrote, almost poetically, of his experiences there:

"One minute it's pitch dark, then the next, it's like a full moon is lighting up the cloudless sky. And moments later my rifle is burning my hand it's so hot. I remember asking God to please not let it jam on me. The target was everywhere and anything that moved. Every few minutes dirt was in my eyes from enemy bullets that kicked up dirt as they struck within inches of my face. In the heat of the fight, I could smell the Chinks' breath. Some of them looked like they were drunk, the way they staggered around firing their weapons…. Every so often one of them would charge right at our position, falling dead within feet of our bunker…. At daybreak, we found the whole mountaintop to be covered with dead bodies, theirs, and ours—only more of theirs. [Even so] we may have had more planes, bombs, and long-range artillery, but they had more manpower than we, and less fear of dying."

Yet, even within this maelstrom of equal opportunity killing and dying, there was little manifestation of a blood brotherhood. Recalling the old stereotype of the "Bug-Out Division," he wrote:

"In the early days of the war, I understand, there was plenty of bugging out. Joe Chink would blow his bugles or fire his burp guns, and our boys would drop their weapons and bug out. At least that's what some of the old-timers told me when I joined the Deuce-Four. They said it was common practice by all UN forces…but of course the all-black, Puerto Rican, and South Korean units were the ones usually singled out when it came to the blaming. Well, I missed all that. By the time I was assigned to the outfit in December 1951, it was *fight or die*."

You had to have that mind-set. There was no option: Fight or die. Period. Even racism paled to being in mortal peril. When Curtis pined to go home, his sergeant mused that he might have "second thoughts" dealing with "Whitey" and Jim Crow back home. Curtis's response was direct: "Can't nothing be as bad as combat, Sarge."

He was right. Nonetheless, again, like me, Curtis was tainted, and it led to him being court-martialed as well when his hitch was over, and he returned home. The charge was disobeying an order. He, too, admitted to the charge, but told the military court it was because he had been singled out, sent on demeaning KP duty—kitchen patrol—three times a week. I had also acted out of principle, to give a little more rest to weary, dog-tired troops in training. Neither of us prevailed, our arguments falling on deaf ears. White ears. Curtis got it much worse. Unlike me, his conviction was not overturned. He was sentenced to solitary confinement in the Fort Leonard Wood stockade for five days, then four months back in prison. Undeterred from service, he reenlisted and was stationed in Japan.

As the war ground to a standoff, the Chinese continued to beef up the North Korean forces, and launched attacks in the south, while we fought terribly costly defensive battles. The enemy lost twice as many men as we did, but they were fanatically dedicated. And, for me, war was now far removed from a romantic quest for bravery and identity. Having been sent back with physical and psychological wounds that ran deep, I was in no way able to function as a soldier. I returned to the front lines and stayed for one night, and one night only. I was too frightened to stay. I was shell shocked. I couldn't deny it; I couldn't hide it. In my moments of coherence and bravado, I could seem the same guy who had been first to volunteer for a suicide mission, but when shooting began and my mind returned back to that night of horror, hell, and biblical visions, I lived in cold, earthly fear.

In truth, I should have been back home being treated for lingering nightmares and self-doubts. I knew that I would eventually get better, but I was not the same guy. I didn't need to be told I had a case of PTSD—or what was euphemistically called "battle fatigue." I didn't need to be told my brain was addled, and that there was a real risk of me losing my grip on life—or my trigger-finger. I was now the archetypal bad soldier. The losing soldier. The useless soldier. I tried to hide it, but my officers could see through any pretense. Finally, taking pity on me, and perhaps recognizing the egregious error that had been made in Yokohama to return me to Korea, my superiors pulled me from the front, and the very next day I was on my way back to Japan. I wasn't all that eager to get back to the States. I was extremely proud of what we, as soldiers, were doing, and how we acquitted ourselves. My family—and my country for that matter—knew little or nothing about what was going on overseas. Leaving Korea, I was in another dimension, like the Twilight Zone, of sight, sound, and mind. But I could eventually put the pieces together and feel a wave of relief that I had done my job and could redirect my life to its next stage.

This was a feeling soon shared by scores of soldiers who were to catch a break when people in Washington gave up the ghost, including President Dwight Eisenhower, who had promised in his campaign that he would personally visit Korea. By the time he returned, he wisely understood that not even a general of his wisdom could have altered the course of this war. And so he gave the order to sign an armistice. It was signed in July 1953, as a tie, a permanent stalemate, though the Chinese could, and did, boast about holding the United States to a draw, establishing themselves as a new world power.

War. Was it the most significant—most impactful event ever to occur in my life? I do not know. I can say it has had the most lasting impact. The toll of war on a combat soldier cannot be measured in blood or pain, nor even life or death. Rather, it is in the lingering war of self-pride versus self-doubt in currents and crosscurrents driven by morality, amorality, and immorality. All one knew before of righteousness was necessarily stripped of essential meaning in order to succeed as a soldier, a fighting machine, a killer trained by one's government. A soldier troubled by concepts like guilt and shame is a worthless soldier, and worthless soldiers are losing soldiers, captured or dead soldiers.

One is expected to be programmed for barbarity, then deprogrammed for the normal modes of society. But humans don't work that way. Society has hidden behind terms such as "post-traumatic stress disorder" to characterize the repressed emotions of fighting men who cannot turn off their messed-up psyches like a light switch. We can keep nursing our wounds as best we can; we tell the mind we're healed and those things will get better. But the conscience has no bandage.

The lucky ones avoid the direct fire and fury. I am among the unlucky ones. Lucky to be alive; but unlucky to have been in the bowels of hell and wounded in body and mind, both bothersome to this day—to this very minute, to be frank. I can maneuver around it, walk on the tightrope of normalcy with a limp and accomplish goals, live dreams, though I have the advantage and burden of being able to write about the unimaginable carnage of being enmeshed in and the aftermath of a long night in hell.

In the end, Korea, to some, was a war without reason or rhyme, a three-year carnage that marked a new era of warfare, one of "containment," not victory, a war of choice rather than necessity, a war of vague justification— indeed, even the very nomenclature changed for such misadventures, from "war" to "conflict." Another such undeniable waste of blood, treasure, and lives would come around the next decade, with even more humiliation for America.

As MacArthur had learned, to his dismay, all the firepower and advantage in the world, cannot conquer the hearts and minds of people ready and willing to die for their precepts of nationalism. That reality would make me question my own assumptions about being a soldier. And, in a strong sense, while hardly putting myself on the same plane as Douglas MacArthur, both he and I were victims of that now almost-forgotten war, which terminated military service for each of us. For the old general, it was cause for him to simply fade away. For me, it was the basis to begin a new life, with no inkling how many roads that would take me down.

Troop ship home

WESTERN UNION

W. P. MARSHALL, PRESIDENT

R.WA584 LONG RX. GOVT PD=FAX WASHINGTON DC 1952 AUG 29 PM 5 17

MRS ANNA MCEACHIN=

THE SECRETARY OF THE ARMY HAS ASKED ME TO EXPRESS HIS DEEP
REGRET THAT THE WOUNDS RECEIVED BY YOUR SON PFC MCEACHIN
JAMES E. JR IN KOREA ON 14 AUG 52 ACCORDING TO AN
ADDITIONAL REPORT ARE OF A SERIOUS NATURE CONSISTING OF
SHELL FRAGMENTS PENETRATING THE ABDOMEN AND RIGHT THIGH
WITH OTHER WOUNDS OF THE LIVER PERIOD ADDRESS MAIL QUOTE
RANK NAME SERVICE NUMBER 141ST GENERAL HOSPITAL APO 1005
CARE POSTMASTER SAN FRANCISCO CALIFORNIA UNQUOTE=

WM E BERGIN MAJOR GENERAL USA THE ADJUTANT GENERAL OF
THE ARMY=

THE COMPANY WILL APPRECIATE SUGGESTIONS FROM ITS PATRONS CONCERNING ITS SERVICE

CHAPTER 4

IT'S MIDNIGHT AGAIN

In the summer of 1953, with an egregious toll taken on both sides, the war ended. North Korea and the United Nations signed an armistice. South Korea refused to sign it, but rather than push on in bloody, senseless carnage, everyone pretty much wanted to just get the hell out of there, including yours truly. With tiny bits of shrapnel embedded in my gut, my lungs still burning from the toxic sewage I had inhaled and my mind suffering gaps in memory, I was part of a massive assembly of humanity bundled onto the Navy transport ship *Marine Adder* for a seasick-inducing trek across the Pacific. Every square inch of it was occupied by soldiers, most of whom probably had their future lives charted. Not me. I had trained, physically and mentally, to be a soldier for life. Indeed, it was the only life I knew.

I had a lot of time on the *Adder* to think. The trip seemed longer and more discomfiting than that of the USS *James O'Hara* when it brought me to Korea a couple of years earlier. To be sure, those intervening years had a deep, profound effect on my outlook, my powers of reasoning, my very innocence. Back when I enlisted, I felt that, as the gospel song goes, I had the whole world in my hands. Now, I was just another GI with war ravages, my memory blocking events I had a right to know about, sitting on the deck of a floating tin can.

When the *Adder* finally came into port in Seattle, a large crowd of the soldiers' families and friends waited on the dock, along with local citizens who cheered as we disembarked. Although my own family could not make the trip from faraway New Jersey, I felt a surge of pride that people were there thanking us for our service. We had heard that the country had been barely paying attention to the unpopular war, and that that small show of support on the dock in Seattle was an exception; most of the soldiers returned to little affection, a far cry from the wild celebrations that awaited the men who fought World War II. There was no V-K Day, no crowds filling Times Square, no nurses kissing sailors in the street.

This was the virtual blueprint for the end of the even more unpopular war in Vietnam two decades later, a new turn in the course of American culture as it related to the military—and one reason why I am a tireless messenger of the cause of honoring our veterans. For me, keeping the fire burning for those men year-round is infinitely more meaningful than parades, Memorial Day, a day that is little more than a merchandising gimmick for stores to boost stores bottom-lines. Those men fought and died for our very existence, for a cause that rises within me each time I salute the flag. At the same time, having been separated from America for the better part of six years, I didn't know what to expect, and centrally, whether America had changed or was still caught up in the same old web of bigotry and selective advancement.

Yet, given my commitment to service, I was still committed to the military. My idealism in serving my country with honor was inviolate. I was a Silver Star honoree. And with my second honorable discharge soon to be finalized, I believed a little downtime would recharge my batteries and dissolve any effects of my battle fatigue, allowing me to then resume my career as a soldier with the rank of an officer. As with my first discharge three years before, I could again enlist and attend officer training school. As the demobilization of the troops proceeded—with thousands to be left in Korea, where to this day we still send young men in uniform to protect the South—I would hold the rank of staff sergeant back at Fort Dix, supervising the training of new soldiers. Technically, my status was "on leave," not "retired."

My immediate objective was to simply get back to Hackensack. The itinerary was to fly across the country in a series of connecting military flights. However, when we arrived, there was terrible news. A military transport plane carrying discharged soldiers had crashed, killing something like forty men. Accidents of this kind had been happening with alarming frequency, and so the government decided to immediately ground all such flights within the U.S. That meant I would take a bus for the slow, torturous cross-county journey. We would need to stop along the way at hotels for the night. The first stop was in Butte, Montana. There were a few of us black guys on the bus. When we went into a hotel, we were told we couldn't stay there. It mattered not to the people at the front desk that they were denying beds to soldiers wearing the uniform of the United States Army, who had served honorably.

That's when I knew I was back in America.

Nothing seemed to have changed. Just before I had shipped out to Korea, I had been arrested in Maywood, New Jersey, by white cops for allowing a buddy of mine, who we called Big Billy, to drive my mother's powder blue 1949 DeSoto. Big Billy wanted to have some time with his girlfriend, a gal named Ruth. I told him to go ahead, but that he had to take me along. We were driving through the white Maywood section of Paterson, where if you were black, the saying went, "You better stay off the street if you don't wanna draw the heat." (Bob Dylan would use these words in his 1975 ballad, *Hurricane.*) Big Billy had had a few drinks that night, so when the cops pulled us over, they busted him for drunk driving and driving without a license. I had to pay a fine of fifty dollars and five dollars in court costs for letting him take the wheel. Billy went to jail for thirty-five days!

Had it been white folks in that car, the cops would have winked and said, "Have a good night, boys." The whole point of busting us was to send a message—stay out of Maywood. For the most part, that message was received by every black person in northern New Jersey. Hell, a few years later, they framed Hurricane Carter, the middleweight boxer, for murder and stuck him in jail for almost twenty years after busting him on just such a drive through Paterson.

So now, fast forward three years. I was far from New Jersey, in the heart of the rural northwest. Yet it may as well have been Maywood. I was wearing the uniform of the United States and being denied a room by white people who had not lifted a finger to fight for America. There was a black soldier in our group named McCarthy who was a real rabble-rouser, a troublemaker. It didn't take much to set him off. He began mouthing off to the manager of the place, putting him to shame, getting right up into the guy's face. The situation was resolved when some of the white soldiers took our side and the hotel employees backed down. It was a small, historically obscure crack in the brick-and-mortar wall of racism, but nonetheless, it was proof that black men would not accept being second-class anymore, that we had moved the ball down the field in a movement that would soon coalesce into a cause.

I would like to say that my family gave me a hero's welcome, but I'd be lying. The truth is, they were blasé about it. I was given about the same level of respect that I was given before I served, which is to say, not much. Nobody cared. What's more, nobody seemed to know I was a wounded veteran; no stories about it appeared in the local papers; nobody in the barber shops spent hours talking about it. At home, I was just another body around the house, hogging a bed and eating the food. But then, I figured I'd be serving somewhere in the world in uniform before long.

Once back at Fort Dix, I cruised along, making no waves. I performed my duties as a training instructor. I received the news that I had been awarded another ribbon—the Republic of Korea's Presidential Unit Citation Badge, which I believed would enhance my credentials when I applied for a commission. As I waited and waited for word of that from above, I decided I couldn't wait any longer and took a civil service test to see if I qualified for a job outside the military. When the scores came back, even I was surprised by how well I had done. It even got a mention in the papers. One reported, "James E. McEachin, Jr., of 190 Central Avenue, a Korean veteran, placed second on the police Civil Service lists and third on the fire list."

And so, on September 15, 1954, I traded in one uniform for another. By then, my discharge came in and I knew the military was no longer an option; I was never going to be commissioned. I had received the payment one got when discharged and went down to Newark shopping for clothes. All I had worn for six years were Army uniforms. I didn't even have a pair of socks or underwear that weren't issued by a quartermaster. I put the khakis away and bought a real sharp gray suit for forty dollars and strutted around for a while, which must have impressed the ladies. Alma, the girl whose picture was stolen while I was in the hospital in Yokohama, had married some homeless guy named Harold. I met a wonderful girl named Lois Davis, a great girl from a good and decent family, and we quickly grew serious. Things were going along well—a black version of the '50s American Dream.

When I had finally given up hope for a commission, I faced a conundrum: Should I be a cop or a fireman? And here is where ingrained, conditioned racism entered my life's path again. The fact was, racism was pervasive in both the fire and police departments; there was a single black firefighter in town at the time, and only a few cops were black. For that reason, I really had no interest in the fire department. I was undeniably better suited for police work, having served as a Military Policeman in Japan and having gotten a certificate in criminology. But then, knowing that I could join either department, the fire chief came to my Aunt Edna's house on First Street in Hackensack where I was living. He hadn't been invited to sit down before he started extolling the virtues of the police department! Then he started telling me all the reasons I shouldn't join the fire department.

"You were injured in Korea, right?" he said. "Well, you won't be able to handle all the physical tests and the stress. You don't want that, do you?"

I knew what he was doing; it was as obvious as a punch in the mouth that he wanted to keep me out of the fire department. As it happened, finishing as high on the civil service exam as I had, they had to come to me. They needed three or four men who had scored high, and the others were white. The fire chief just happened to get there before the police chief and damn, he made being a police officer seem like a stroll in the park. Precisely because I knew he didn't want me in the fire department, I took the job.

"Okay, I'll be a fireman," I told him.

There was only one problem. I hated being a fireman. I didn't get the warmest reception from the other firemen, to put it gently. Oh, I did get a thrill riding on the back of the fire truck, the hook and ladder. But it surprised some of my friends, who would drive by the red brick station house in Hackensack and, seeing me, call out, "Hey, look, it's McEachin. He's a fireman!" Almost everybody knew I didn't belong there, that I needed a bigger challenge. Not that the life of a fireman is uneventful. There was no picnic to be had when the bell rang, only real danger. We had a four-alarm fire early one evening at Petrillo's Everglades, an extremely popular Italian restaurant on Essex Avenue. I hadn't seen flames reaching into the sky like that even in Korea. It devastated the block and filled my already-damaged lungs with thick gray smoke. That night, I said to myself, "Nothing is worse than doing this for a living." I made up my mind.

The next day, I wrote a letter of resignation to the chief of the fire department, telling him I was going to transfer to the Police Department. And his response was, "We hate to lose you, but we want you to be happy, son." That was some real bad acting from the chief. Clearly, he was thrilled. He'd never wanted me, or any other black man, in the department. That's the way it was in Hackensack. The police department wasn't ideal, either, and of course it still isn't. We know the dark history of police brutality against black people. In the urban corridors of northern New Jersey, the legacy of Hurricane Carter lives on as a daily object lesson.

The police force did offer a black man more opportunity than the fire department, but the rarity of it was such that my transition attracted a great deal of public attention. Even though no one knew who I was, *The Bergan Record* ran a story titled "Fireman Gives Up Hose for a Whistle, Nightstick: McEachin Switches to Police Department, Sees Greater Chances for Advancement."

In my own subtle way, I was paving the way for progress. I proved that I could be a good cop, and I really showed my criminology chops. After the New Year of 1955, I was able to make a few arrests of criminals based the bulletins I would review. I would see somebody who matched a description and move in on them. A couple times I identified teenagers walking down the street as missing persons and returned them to their homes, or I would bust someone for reckless driving: small potatoes stuff, but important to the folks who lived in the town. Sometimes, I had to cross my friends.

I also didn't like the numbers racket being carried out on the street or the smalltime hoodlums who would collect on the gambling debts. I took it on myself to bust some of those guys. When they would see me coming, they would scatter like ants. I tried to be a good cop, an honest cop, and my superiors did everything to defang me. Was I a bit too overzealous in my methods? It's a matter of opinion. I never went rogue. I followed the rules, but may have bent a few on occasion, as any good cop must do. I believe this gave the brass an excuse to tame me, and in the hope of eventually getting rid of me.

In March 1955, I took a two-day sick leave. When I returned, I found that a fellow cop, Burgum, had filed a complaint against me for failing to report to duty. A memo came down from no less than Chief of Police William Menke grandly writing, "I find you guilty as charged" and penalizing me the days. The chief must have clenched his jaw as my credits continued to be written up in the papers, and I can only imagine his thoughts when, a year later, I received a letter from the Acting Chief of Police, Westervelt Demarest—who would soon replace Menke, praising my apprehension of car thieves. He wrote:

"I extend greetings and commend you for your alertness, keen observation, and attention to the duty you performed. It therefore gives me pleasure to pass along word of much accomplishment, through official channels to the City Manager, Mayor, and Council."

And yet, I always had the uneasy feeling that the brass was out to get me. After I left the force, I heard that another guy, Bobby, had been murdered. "Too late," I said, comfortable on a train heading west. "I've already moved to California.

It still jars me to look back through the sheaf of papers I saved from those days and see directives from the top of the department referring to black suspects as "colored." This was how ingrained racism worked: through conditioned language. Another manifestation was under-the-radar personnel moves. For example, out of nowhere—and right after I had gotten that letter of commendation—I received notice that I was being transferred from headquarters to the Traffic Division! Instead of solving crimes and arresting the bad guys, I would be writing traffic tickets.

To my way of thinking, it was the lowest form of police work, essentially on the same level as being a school crossing guard. There was no explanation, and it was to be temporary. But I had no intention of accepting it, even for a day. Apparently, Demarest agreed. When he heard my appeal, he sent word to City Manager Harold Reilly that upended the plan. And so, I was back on the beat—and into the thick of controversy. In November of 1956, my work indirectly shed light on another cop's misconduct. The cop, Reedy Evans, was charged with tipping off the owner of Club 20, a man named George Foster, who had been illegally selling booze without a license. Evans, upon learning that the authorities were closing in, warned Foster, "Clean up your own backyard—the State A.B.C. agents are in town," referring to agents from Alcohol and Beverage Control. How did the department know he had warned Foster? From me. I had learned about it from a confidential source, upon which I informed Chief Demarest and Detective Sergeant John Conforti. I knew Reedy, and I loved his wife, Ruthie. But Reedy was the craziest cop I ever knew. Once, after he drew a sketch of a criminal, the police artist told him it was terrible. "Well," Reedy replied, "I ain't no architect." He had even beaten a man to death on the job in 1952, but the murder charge against him was dismissed. It was his decision to tip off Foster and that was his undoing, not me. At his trial, Reedy claimed that I lied about him, but the jig was up. He was found guilty and temporarily suspended.

That was sad, but it was a mere warm-up for the next incident on my agenda, one that demonstrated the extreme perils and terror a cop can face, with no forewarning.

At around 2:30 in the morning of February 23, 1957, I was in my patrol car riding around the darkened streets of Hackensack, when a call from dispatch crackled on my radio requesting immediate backup for Patrolman Al Carlson. He had gotten a call about a suspected break-in on Rowland Avenue. When he arrived at the scene, he spotted a man, later identified as twenty-five-year-old college student Donald Reno, jumping from the porch. Bolting from his cruiser, Carlson began to chase the guy through the back- yards of the houses on the block.

He fired two warning shots in the air and shouted for Reno to halt. When he kept scurrying through the yards, Carlson radioed for help. I floored it and got to the scene within a minute, as did three other cops. All of us gave chase. After five minutes or so, we thought we had lost him. Then, guns drawn, in the dead of night, we heard the telltale rattling of a garbage can in the yard behind a house between Simons and Sutton Avenues. We carefully inched through the alley. Suddenly,

Carlson saw the silhouette of a man and shined his flashlight on him. We could see the whites of Reno's eyes for a split-second before he sprang up like a quicksilver jack rabbit and scurried out of the yard. Carlson and another cop fired their guns. In all, six shots went flying through the night air, the sky lighting up with the fire that spit from their gun barrels. There was no order, only chaos—a fury of sight and sound that was instantly familiar to me. It was Korea all over again. In fact, just for a moment, I had but one thought: God help me, it's midnight again.

Although Reno was hit, he was running on adrenaline and kept going, charging through the alley. I took pursuit right behind him, disregarding the possibility of more shots being fired in the dark. He emerged on the street in front of 464 Sutton Avenue. When I got close enough, I threw my body headlong at him and brought him down with a flying tackle as good as any pro football player. In hindsight, this was a remarkably similar situation to the outrageous police killing of Rayshard Brooks in Atlanta in June 2020, shot in the back as he fled on foot; while I could have fired on Reno, as the white Atlanta cop had on Brooks, my instinct told me to apprehend, not kill. That was one moral conundrum I was spared.

As I subdued Reno, sitting on top of him as I cuffed him, blood oozed from his back where he had been hit. He was weak, his voice quavering and breathless, but he managed to speak.

"Take me to the hospital," he said.

A second later, as he lost consciousness, his last words escaped.

"Let me die."

An ambulance arrived and Reno was carried onto it and taken to Hackensack Hospital, barely alive, in critical condition. The bullet that entered his back caused terrible damage. His stomach and diaphragm were perforated, and he had lost a great deal of blood. As you can imagine, the story was given front-page treatment: "Police Bullets Stop Break-in; Hackensack Man Near Death," read the headline in *The Bergen Record*. I and the other cops were advised not to speak to the press, for legal reasons. Meanwhile, Reno lasted eight days, during which he underwent a tracheotomy to allow him to breathe easier. Then, without ever regaining consciousness, he died on March 4.

Reno had lived in the neighborhood, and in the aftermath of the episode his family presented a counter-narrative. They insisted he hadn't broken into the house, that he had come from seeing a movie and was simply taking a shortcut through neighbors' yards so he could enter his house through the back door. However, that excuse fell apart, as Reno's house was two blocks away. He had also been reported missing for two days. That and other inconsistencies would be noted by the defense attorney when the family filed a $200,000 wrongful death suit against Patrolman Carlson and the City of Hackensack. During the trial, not just Carlson but all of us who had responded to the call that night endured slings and arrows.

Friends of Donald Reno claimed he was "a fine young man" and that Carlson was immature, poorly trained, and mentally unfit to carry a firearm. It was alleged that the police were trigger-happy, that they were hiding certain details of the shooting from the public. Their case was that a "great injustice" had been done. The case went to a grand jury, the final determination of which was that we had acted in accordance with police procedure; the result was "justifiable homicide." No indictments. The case was dismissed.

I realize that reasonable people can disagree, but when a man runs from police as Reno did, he forfeits any claim of innocence. I had no inner anguish about it, but that is what bothers me the most. I didn't say, "We shot this guy, and maybe we didn't need to. We had him outnumbered. He couldn't go anywhere." But in truth, I felt nothing. And that, in looking back, scares me. It meant there was a certain part of me that had lost its humanity, that was dead. Combine that with my suspicions about the department plotting against me, and I didn't come away from that night in any better mood. Some things about what happened are a blur, such as whether Reno had a gun and fired at me as I chased him, and whether I shot at him.

I attribute this to my subconscious mind shielding my conscious mind. It really was midnight in Korea again, for a mind that could not bear to deal with sights and sounds of fatal conflict. The result was to blank them out. I could not even force myself to go back to the scene of the crime. Around the same time, I was also having physical problems, a result of my war wounds. My lungs, particularly, were bothering me because they would sometimes fill with fluid, causing me to gasp for breath. Walking my beat, I was coughing all the time. Even back in May of 1955, I had been having problems. I had gone to the policeman's ball that year and blacked out. I came to and decided to undergo a physical, believing I may have sustained a head injury. Instead, when the doctor gave me an electroencephalogram test, the results came back "unsatisfactory."

The bottom line was I had tuberculosis and would at some point need to have an operation—a lobectomy, the removal of one lobe of an infected lung, which prevents the spread of TB. I put the surgery on hold, foolishly. I had joined the fire and then police department; I had taken physicals and come through just fine. There were no psychological exams back then; mostly, they didn't care about your mental state, and barely about your physical state. But I figured I was good enough to let it go. But now, I was coughing up blood regularly, my sputum covered in red. One day, I could not muster up the breath to let me walk across the street. I called headquarters and told them, "You better get somebody over here right away to take over for me."

They sent a car to pick me up and take me home. The patrolman who picked me up, upon seeing my condition, said, "You better go to the doctor." I did, and the doc said, "Mr. McEachin, you need to go to the hospital. Right now." When I was taken to Hackensack Hospital, where Donald Reno had died, as part of the treatment they stuck tubes down my throat. Once I was feeling better, I left and went back to my police work rather than go ahead with the operation. In July 1957, though, the condition flared up again and I checked myself into another hospital, this time at Fort Drum, in Castle Point, New York, where I could keep it all under wraps. Again, once I felt better, I went back to work.

Even so, my lung was ever deteriorating. I couldn't hold off on the operation any longer, and the decision was made by Fate where I would have the procedure done. As I was walking my beat on a bitterly cold night in October, it began snowing—hard—little bits of ice slapping my face. Fate can be funny. That night, I turned on the TV at home and Mike Wallace on his *Interview* show was interviewing

Walter O'Malley, owner of Brooklyn Dodgers about moving the team from Brooklyn to Los Angeles. He went on about how beautiful the weather was out there, the sun, the palm trees. And before the night was done, I was packing my bags. Just days before, I had bought a car, a Lincoln. I took it back to the automobile lot where I had bought it and told the guy I wanted to sell it back. I took the deal he offered me and went right to the Newark train station, bought a ticket, and was on the next train to Los Angeles.

I didn't resign or request a leave of absence from the department. In fact, I said not a word of what I was doing to my family or to the department. The only one I told was Lois. I went to her house that night and explained what I was doing. Bless her heart, she was such a sweet girl. She didn't question me, and I didn't tell her about the operation because it would have worried her to death. I told her I would get settled out there, wherever I was going, then send for her to come and join me.

"You've got my word," I said.

"I know I do," she said. "I know I do."

Great gal that she was, she supported me a thousand percent. She knew it would make me happy to get away from all the garbage I had been going through, said she knew I would succeed at whatever I chose to do. Those were the exact words I needed to hear. I'll go further than that: It was she who got me through that difficult time in my life, and I think that was when I really fell in love with her.

As a veteran, I could rely on the benefits I had earned. When I got to California, I checked in to the VA Hospital in San Fernando out in the San Fernando Valley, and the portion of my lung that had been so debilitated in Korea was finally removed. During my six-month recovery, as I lay in my cramped bed, medication for TB pumping through my veins, my optimism began to grow that I would soon be as good as new. Finally, I got around to writing a letter to the Hackensack Police Department submitting my resignation. I never felt so good about anything in my life. In fact, the trials, and tribulations of being a cop would be the basis for my book *Say Goodnight to the Boys in Blue*, a semi-satirical novel of New Jersey cops—for which I had to change the name of Hackensack to Hilton Head, for legal reasons. They wouldn't have been thrilled by it in Hackensack.

I then called Lois and told her the whole story. She had kept the secret of my exodus to California. I still was not eager to open up to my mother. Then Lois called me, crying, one day early in the new year: My mother had died. By then, I was healthy enough to get out of bed, but the doctors warned me not to travel extensively. A cross-country train ride for a guy who had just had part of his lung removed was insanity, but I had to get back to Hackensack for my mother's funeral. In fact, the funeral of my mother was likely the only reason they would have allowed me to do it. In early March, the doctors gave me a fifteen-day leave from treatment. When I got back to New Jersey, it was—what else? —snowing. Breathing in that cold air, my chest felt like it was in a vise, the pain excruciating. I was coughing, my mucus again bloody. But I got through it. I buried my mother, said a sad goodbye to her, and headed back to California.

I sent for Lois shortly thereafter. She was a devout Christian and wouldn't live in sin, so I swallowed hard and popped the question. When she arrived, I had been released from the hospital and was living in Pacoima, a seven-square-mile patch of arid land and clear streams in the northern part of the San Fernando Valley. I was renting one of those wooden, one-story, fragile homes seemingly erected in about ten minutes, but for a guy with limited resources, it was a nice place to build a nest. Before I carried Lois over the threshold, we went right down the coast to Tijuana to get married on June 25, 1958. She then moved in, sent for her things back in New Jersey, and we would stay together until her passing in July of 2017.

Lois McEachin was a solid, beautiful, magnificent southern-bred soul who tolerated me, not that I ever knew why. She was a major reason why I would flourish because her love and belief in me was unconditional, even though back then I had no job and no real vision of what I should be doing. But remember about fate being funny: One afternoon during my idleness, I turned on the TV and there was some sort of dance party on. Maybe it was Dick Clark's American Bandstand. A wild looking guy was gyrating around on the floor singing or trying to. I stared for a while, disbelieving. "What in the world is that?" I asked Lois.

She patiently explained that it was a hit song, that rock and roll was the in thing, making people money. In fact, just down the road in Pacoima, Richard Valenzuela, the seventeen-year-old son of Mexican parents, was singing with a local band and soldering native Chicano music into the fabric of rock. I didn't know him, but he was en route to a meteoric, tragically brief career as the teen idol called Ritchie Valens. Trying to see what it was that the guy on the TV was doing, I remained mystified.

"That's music?" I said, incredulous. Then, putting on a show of audacity, I added, "Hell, I can do that."

I didn't say how. Because I didn't have a clue. I knew next to nothing about rock and roll, couldn't read or write music, couldn't sing it, couldn't play an instrument, had never bought any rock and roll records. But my reflexive reaction wasn't totally bravado. I knew a bit about rhythm and blues, and I had a way with words. Lois just sort of rolled her eyes. But it was as plausible a career as any other I could think of at the time. Besides, once I get it in my head to do something, I seemed to be able to get it done. That was a gift, and sometimes it could be a curse.

My Mother, Anna

CHAPTER 5

THE BALLAD OF JIMMY MACK

The first song I wrote was called "Tuff Enuff." People have told me this was of historical note because of the phonetically spelled, (some would say "ghettoized," title), an approach that would later become common in funk music, such as in Sly and the Family Stone's mondegreen "Thank You (Falettinme Be Mice Elf Agin)." Hey, I was ahead of my time. For me, it was just how people spoke in my world, how they sounded, and I thought it would hit the eye with a stronger effect. I wasn't aware that I was being inventive. There have since been several songs with this title, spelled the same way, including a top-ten hit in 1986 by The Fabulous Thunderbirds, the Texas blues-rock band. I suppose I should be flattered that the idea was mine— not least of all because it was recorded by none other than Otis Redding. As I recall, the words and music came easily to me. The opening went like this:

"Woke up this mornin' and I heard the news.

They shootin' at the moon and gonna blow the fuse.

Shootin' three-stage rockets through the universe.

And some say the whole thing's gonna get worse.

Gettin' rough, yeah. Tuff enuff."

Some explanation: At the time, the country was all a-flutter about the space race between America and Russia. This was late 1959, at the height of the Cold War. People were freaking out when the Sputnik satellite success- fully completed its orbit around Earth, the worry was that Russia would own the universe. The paranoia hung in the air. I thought, hey, what better way to cash in on it than write a song about it? No one else had. I used it as the backdrop for a song really about a guy who wanted to believe he was tough but was just "poor ole me with no hidin' place" when all hell would break loose and kill us all. There was a little more complexity to it than the typical superficial rock-and-roll fodder on the radio. It had to rock, so I set it to a funky shuffle beat I took from the Coasters, who were racking up big hits. You had to make the kids want to dance. That was rule one. It wasn't half bad, I must say. A little Coasters here, a smidgeon of Little Richard there. When I had completed it, the next step was to try to sell it to a song publisher. I didn't know a single one.

However, Pacoima was getting attention in the newspapers because of Ritchie Valens, more so after he tragically perished on February 3rd that year in a plane crash with Buddy Holly and the Big Bopper. I learned that Ritchie had recorded for a label called Del-Fi, owned by Bob Keane. I looked up the address; like many of the independent labels around L.A., it was on Selma Avenue. I then went down there and said I had a song— as did probably ten thousand other people in town. But I had a certain cockiness to me that came naturally. I could talk my way into offices and found myself in Bob's.

I had no recorded demo of the song to play for him, which was standard procedure. I didn't know music theory, couldn't even read notes, so I went to a transcription service and sang it for him to chart a lead sheet. Even with a voice that sounded like a rusty gate, Bob liked it enough to buy it. I don't remember for how much, for a pittance, I'm sure. But what did I care? It was a score, on the first try. What I didn't realize was that the real payoff in the music business was on the publishing end. Bob, like the other label owners, had his own publishing company, Kemo Music. For almost nothing, he secured the publishing rights in perpetuity on whatever sales the record would accrue. The artists themselves were paid like peons at a half-cent per record sold. Of course, as the songwriter—as Jimmy McEachin—I would prosper on sales, because the numbers were charted not by the labels, but the BMI accounting firm.

I didn't think it would be too difficult for Bob to find a singer and cut the song. L.A. at the time was a bustling music colony, with records being made every day at rudimentary studios for labels big and small, which existed as an answer to the New York labels, like Columbia and RCA. The "big beat" could be heard nonstop on transistor radios, in cars, and on jukeboxes in the plethora of dance clubs on the Strip. Within the recording industry hierarchy, Capitol was at the top and, down the ladder, Imperial, Specialty, Challenge, and Liberty. Many of these began as jazz and R&B outlets, and still were, but the priority was rock and roll, which took the industry by storm in the mid-50s. In addition to longtime popular singers, like Frank Sinatra at Capitol (soon to jump to his own label, Reprise), most of the popular doo-wop groups came from this colony. The biggest acts in rock—Fats Domino, Little Richard, the Platters, the Penguins, Sam Cooke, Jesse Belvin, Larry Williams—recorded for the L.A. labels. Del-Fi may not have been in that stratum, but Ritchie had made it a force. The L.A. sound was looser, more daring, more amenable to unknown writers than what was coming out of the Brille Building in New York. And so, I waited for that big break . . . and kept waiting.

As I did, I continued to write songs. Among the titles was a semi spoken song with a Coasters-like riff called "Gravel Gert." Women's names in song titles were a popular gimmick—the twist was that Gravel Gert was "ugly . . . a sorry sight to meet . . . a brand-new chick [who] sure looks sick." Another one, "The Fight," had a spoken intro—call it a proto-rap, if you like—about a title fight between "Heavy Hittin' Henry and Wee Willie Winkle," the underdog who knocked out Henry with "a mighty blow." Others were "Isn't That Right," "I Think of You," "One More Day," and "This Too Shall Live Forever." I would write them about Lois, for she was my muse. I'd either write them trying to sell them or write them specifically for a publisher or record company who asked me to. I would copyright them under either Jim McEachin or Jimmy Mack, have note sheets made, then knock on more doors—and wait for something to happen.

Some things of note did happen. In September 1959, I produced "The Fight" and "Gravel Gert" with a group called the Barons, recorded it with a bandleader named Bruce Locke, and sold it and all the rights to a small label, Demon, run by arranger Joe Greene. Demon was distributed by Liberty Records, which took the Olympics' "Western Movies" into the top ten. Screamin' Jay Hawkins was also on the label, so it had some juice.

When the record came out in October, *Billboard*'s "Reviews of New Pop Records," gave both sides three stars for "Very Strong Sales Appeal" as "Coasters-type" songs. As it turned out, the sales appeal wasn't as strong as Billboard predicted; in February, I got a check from the publisher for—get ready—twenty-five bucks. Well, it was a start. Most records don't make a cent.

By the new decade, Lois had given birth to our two daughters, Felecia and Alainia—I named them so their initials would be F. M. and A. M. Needing more space, and to situate myself closer to the hub of the music scene, I moved us to a walk-up apartment on a quiet side street named Manhattan Place south of Adams Street, down in South Central L.A. It was still a peaceful residential, middle-class area, a good decade before economic starvation turned it into a breeding ground for the drug trade and gang violence, a virtual billboard for the Crips and Bloods—as well as the police beating of Rodney King. The Olympics lived in the complex, as well as the songwriting team of Fred Smith and Cliff Goldsmith (writers of "Hully Gully," "Western Movies," and "Harlem Shuffle") and a lot of music people settled there, so I made a few contacts. One was an exceptionally talented young songwriter, Jackie Avery, who came from Macon, Georgia, to L.A. trying to peddle his own songs. We began noodling around on songs. And while nothing came of it, it was through Jackie that "Tuff Enuff" would find its voice—and what a voice, one that would become the very core of soul music.

In the late summer of 1960, there was a knock on the door. I opened it, and there was Jackie with a big, well-built young man he said he wanted me to meet. Jackie said the guy could sing like nobody's business, could blow the doors off, and only needed the right song to make him a star. The big guy smiled, and when he saw the electric piano in my living room littered with pages of sheet music, he immediately began sifting through them, singing bits and pieces of them. I told him I had a group and needed a lead singer for a song I had—which was "Tuff Enuff"—and he piped up, "I can sing it." He was obviously a man who didn't want to waste even a minute of time. He was hungry for success.

"Anything I can get you?" I asked him.

He continued rifling through the sheet music. "Yeah," he said in a faint Southern accent. "More songs."

Otis Redding was only eighteen at the time, but so fully formed that I assumed he was older. He had the presence of a confident man who'd been around the block. He was obviously ambitious, having roamed two thousand miles from home that summer to live in L.A. with relatives while he tried to find the right path for his talent. His energy seemed endless; when he was in a room, he dominated it. He was a real nice kid, never arrogant, always courtly. Lois loved him. She never cared much for the music crowd, or at least not the musicians I would invite up to noodle songs with on the piano, and she would hide in the bedroom during our jam sessions. She had an innate ability to know who a genuinely good person was and could recognize a leech just out for himself. Otis was about the only one she thought deserved to be in the former category. And she was right.

Jackie apparently had known Otis back in Macon as the big kid followed the trail of that city's two most famous sons in the '50s, Little Richard and James Brown. I knew nothing of his life because he was a closed book. I didn't know his daddy was a minister with whom he had a bumpy relationship because Otis sang the "devil's music." I didn't know he had a young, pregnant wife whom he loved, living on a farm in the Georgia backwoods (and would famously sing about later in the duet he sang with Carla Thomas, "Tramp"). To me, he was one-dimensional, and I do not mean it as a knock. I admired him because he was so driven. He didn't run around like Jackie. He didn't carouse—he would, let's say, accept what Jackie brought for him, but he wasn't on the prowl for booze or women. He was on the prowl for success.

He nailed it on "Tuff Enuff." He and Jackie sang it as a duet and his gruff growling and Avery's high harmony meshed. The verses about the space shots were made less obvious but it flowed as a foot-stomping, finger-popping number. As we went on, he told me that he absolutely worshiped Jackie Wilson, who had reached the heights with "Lonely Teardrops" and "That's Why (I Love You So)," written by Berry Gordy before he founded Motown. I think Otis had met Wilson somewhere back in his past and he wanted to sing like him. I didn't see him in that hue. Although his voice was more powerful than Wilson's, he had a more limited range and wasn't the incredibly athletic showman that the man known as "Mr. Excitement" was. He also idolized Sam Cooke, and I knew Sam well. He would invite me to his Christmas parties, which were swingin.' But Otis was nothing like Sam either, whose voice was velvet.

Otis' was like sandpaper. Soulful sandpaper.

All these guys were natural gospel-blues singers, but Otis was different; he had a growl, his voice emanated from deep within himself, to the point where he would tie himself into knots wringing every last drop of emotion from a song, even when he was just singing in my living room. Later, when he had become a sensation, he sang, "Sad Songs Are All I Know," which was the perfect epitaph for him. But he kept mentioning Wilson so much that I gave in. I tried to accommodate him. We sat at the piano laying down some riffs for a new song, all upbeat and swingin.' Otis wasn't a word man, he was all about the melody, the rhythm, the feel. He could play guitar, which a lot of people don't know, or he would bang on a drum, but it was only to get a tempo.

After "Tuff Enuff," we began noodling around with what was comfortable for him, using the bouncy groove of "That's Why," which had a simple chord structure—not that I knew what those chords were—leaving room for Otis to feel it and veer off on his own. The lyrics I wrote were typically puerile, befitting the era. I started with a Jackie Wilson riff—background singers repeating "uh-uh-huh" and "oh yeah"—about "this little girl, she's so fine" who "got the kind of figure a man can squeeze . . . the kind of love'll make you fall on yo' knees." As we rehearsed it, he sounded uncannily like Wilson but with his own little cadences and sudden mood shifts. Otis didn't just sing lyrics, he owned them, made them uniquely his. He would smother a song, get inside each word. Jackie Avery just naturally pitched in and jammed with us, laying in a smooth background vocal, his high pitch nicely accenting Otis's more untamed vocal. I wanted to use him for the songs, in just that fashion. We called the song "She's All Right."

I had him in the fold for two songs but still needed two more because I wanted four to go into the studio with, as the custom at the time was four sides to a session. I turned to Otis, repeating his words to me.

"Otis," I said, "give me more songs."

He had one that he'd been performing in clubs, "These Arms of Mine," a blues torch song that I believe Jackie Avery wrote. I think Otis hung around with Jackie because he could write, and Otis really could emote on that one, as if his yearning for a woman came straight from the pulpit. Yet, and I say this with some trepidation, I didn't think much of it—again, my judgment is known to be somewhat less than perfect, and in impressively different areas. Making it worse, even now I don't like that song much! I thought he was selling himself short with it. It might have been commercial, but I just didn't like it. I wanted to keep him in that up-tempo groove. I think he was pissed at me for that. But I told him "Gettin' Hip" and "Gamma Lama" were better for him. He, or someone, had written them, and I could lay on a raucous Little Richard style. I loved the line in "Gettin' Hip" that went "Done got hip to your jive," which perfectly summed up that he was wise to the snakes in the industry. Those two songs weren't as promising as the first two. But I wasn't selling songs: I was selling Otis Redding.

Both of us were impatient, but Otis took it up a notch. He was hyper energetic. It was always "Let's go, let's go, let's go." So, I got on my horse and got going. With the songs chosen, I made a rough demo of "She's All Right" and took it to a local radio station, KUDU, in Oxnard, just up the coast from L.A. The disc jockey loved it; he played it something like twenty times that night. That was a harbinger for me; I knew I had something, maybe something big. I couldn't have possibly paid for pressing and distributing enough records to keep that ball rolling, so the next order of business was to feel out the record labels to take a flyer on Otis, lay out money for a recording session, get the four sides down, and then sign him to a contract, with the proviso that I would produce his records.

There was a hitch to my grandiose plan: I had not yet produced an actual record session. But, like songwriting, I didn't see why I couldn't do that job either. I'd hung around studios sucking up the protocols, learning what all those buttons and knobs on the soundboard were for, getting familiar with the studios around town. I had no compunction talking tough and pulling rank in this manner. I was feeling my oats and was quite proprietary about Otis Redding; he had come to me, and I had gotten him on track, harnessing a musical locomotive. One executive was especially receptive to the plan. His name was Al Kavelin, and he was the founder of Lute and Trans World Records, both of which had just begun that summer, enjoying a big hit right out of the box with the Hollywood Argyles' doo-wop spoof "Alley Oop," which had been recorded for twenty-five dollars.

Al Kavelin was a man of distinction. Born in Russia, he immigrated to

America as a child and, in the '30s, led pianist Carmen Cavallaro and the rest of his orchestra in performances at top-shelf clubs and ritzy hotel ballrooms. His partner at Trans World was Morey Bernstein, a classic record-business character with little real understanding of music but an ear for marketable talent. Al depended on Morey's judgment and had me play Otis' demo of "She's All Right" in Morey's office. Because Otis had a way of distorting words according to the groove, sometimes creating brand new words, Morey was a bit puzzled.

"I couldn't understand a word he was singing," he told me.

"It's something called soul," I replied, as patiently as I could.

Morey's sixth sense told him Otis was the real deal, but rather than sign him right there, he wanted to do a trial run, having Otis record the four songs in a formal studio session, to be produced by me. The biggest incentive for me was that Al would pay for it, so I wouldn't need to scrimp on anything. I could go full bore. The details were left to me, and I chose Gold Star Studios on Santa Monica Boulevard in Hollywood. The big stars at the big labels would go to United Studios or Capitol. But Gold Star was a gas— and, not incidentally, cheap. The studio itself was small and cramped but its acoustics were responsible for the thickest, fattest echoes of any studio, amplified even more by eighteen-foot-long, custom-built echo chambers. This was why Bob Keane had Ritchie Valens make all his records there; his words were not sung so much as caressed. Producers got a little crazy at Gold Star, the craziest being Phil Spector in the early and mid-1960s when he erected his "Wall of Sound" around those fabulous echoes.

And so, with the handshake agreement I had with Al Kavelin—just try working on a handshake these days, with billions of dollars on the line and every word hammered out by expensive lawyers—I went to Gold Star with Otis and Jackie, where we met up with a trio of female background singers, the Blossoms, led by the immortal voice of Darlene Love, who would blossom indeed as a Spector act. I was fortunate that Al was not only paying for the time but had the best arranger in the industry, René Hall, who arranged Sam Cooke's sessions, and booked some of the best session musicians in the business—drummers Ed "Sharkey" Hall and Earl Palmer (who backed Fats Domino, Lloyd Price, and Little Richard in sessions in New Orleans), pianist Ernie Freeman, sax man Plas Johnson.

René, along with Ed Redman, had drawn up lead sheets and we rehearsed the songs until I knew what I wanted to hear. Then I turned on the microphones. It was go time.

Otis' voice was clear as a bell, strong, his energy unbounded and infectious. In those days, studios had a prehistoric two-track reel-to-reel tape machine. Stereo recording was for the highbrows, classical or orchestral music. We recorded everything in a fat slab of mono, vocals with the instruments jamming, in every way four live performances, as if in a night- club. Sometimes we could overdub a second horn or another vocal to the mix, but in the main we came out with what we had, mistakes and all. And my mistake was obvious—I hadn't realized it during the session, but had I paid closer attention to the sound pouring from the speakers in the control booth, I would have heard Otis' once-in-a-lifetime voice being stepped on too much by Jackie and the girls. I thought rock and roll had to be loud and wild, and with that Gold Star echo billowing, melding with all the voices, what came out was the sound of a group act, not the debut of Otis Redding. At some intervals, it was hard to distinguish Otis from Jackie, except when Otis branched off into his lofty, soul-exploding improvised moments.

I didn't realize this during the session, and it was too late afterwards to fix it; as it was, I had used up pretty much all the chits that Al had extended. There were not going to be any do-overs. So, I took the tapes to Al and Morey, and they liked what they heard, especially "Tuff Enuff" and "She's All Right," but which they thought sounded too much like a duet to promote Otis alone. Accordingly, they signed both Otis and Jackie, for a hundred dollars apiece. The terms of the contracts were typical—typical BS. Otis and Jackie were given the industry standard of a half-cent royalty per every record sold—damn near indentured servitude. As Little Richard once said, "Whoever heard of cutting a penny in half!" But, like most of the black artists from impoverished families and conditions, for Otis it was a shot at stardom. And for me, a shot at riding a raging bull to prominence in the record industry. It was a pleasant thought, at least. Al would release Otis' first record ever, "She's All Right" backed with "Tuff Enuff," in October 1960, but he hedged by putting it not on Lute but an associated label, Trans World, with both sides originally credited not to Otis but to The Shooters. I argued that Otis should have his name on the record and Al came around halfway. "She's All Right" was credited to "The Shooters featuring Otis Redding"; "Tuff Enuff" went to "The Shooters featuring

Jackie Avery." I think he wanted to see which song did the better business and continue with either Otis or Jackie as the front man. Further complicating the issue, while "Tuff Enuff" was credited to "J. McEachin," "She's All Right" was credited to "O. Redding-J. McEachin." That was not accurate: I wrote both, period. But I was not averse to Otis claiming a writing credit.

The real confusion was over publishing rights. Al wanted to own the rights on all four songs. Publishing was the biggest rip-off; label owners purloined those potentially lucrative rights for themselves, which they could not do with writers' royalties, since those were determined by independent accountants at BMI. A record executive would pay maybe fifty dollars to the writer of a song in exchange for hogging all the future publishing royalties.

Well, I couldn't have sold the publishing rights on "Tuff Enuff," which were held by Bob Keane. As for "She's All Right," I intended to establish my own publishing company, splitting any of those royalties with Otis. So, I retained the publishing on both songs of Otis' debut single. Listen, I didn't futz around. I was serious and smart, and I'm sure Al held it against me. Like in any other industry, black guys weren't supposed to be smart or stand up for themselves. The record business has always exploited that.

We pushed on, with egos and gripes simmering. As we waited to see how the record would sell and it became clear that Al and Morey weren't prepared to spend the money necessary to get it played. Hell, I did better with a demo pitching it myself. "She's All Right" died out of the gate. Perhaps the record had flaws, but it was unmistakably the work of a rare artist, a magnetic blues rocker who was just a little ahead of his time.

Otis and I were quite disappointed, and within days I found out that he had suddenly left L.A. and gone back to Macon with Jackie Avery, I believe. That came after Al and Morey decided not to even release the two other Otis Redding songs they had, a decision that may have hastened Lute and Trans World going out of business by mid-decade. I couldn't say I was surprised Otis left with no warning. That was how Otis rolled; he was antsy. He knew he would happen, but not how or when or with whom. His exit didn't change my deep-seated belief that he would one day be a commanding figure in music. But I do admit that I was hurt. Hurt and angry.

Of course, it was the right thing. He found context and respect in Memphis with Stax/Volt— "Soulsville, USA." I need not be reminded that when he had his audition there, the song he sang was "These Arms of Mine." He still believed in the song, and he was right. And if Jackie Avery wrote it, he too woke up one day and saw his name taken off it; the song is credited only to Otis. But Jackie found his niche, too, writing songs for Otis' protege Arthur Conley. I never did hear from either again. I was told that when Otis came to L.A. a few years later he asked about me, but we didn't connect. His triumphs were many: His appearances, such as the one at the Monterey Pop Festival, and albums, such as "Otis Blue", set a new standard for soul that could grab you and hold on until he sang the last note. But sadly, success came with a toll. His last song, in 1967, famously and heartbreakingly confessed: "I have nothing to live for, looks like nothing's gonna come my way." Days later, his plane went down in a lake in Wisconsin.

Despite all the remembrances that were given after Otis' sudden death, no one seemed to know that Otis had made his first recordings at Gold Star, produced by Jimmy McEachin, backed by Darlene Love. For me, those memories are still magical. Though my copyright on "She's All Right" has long expired and been sold off. But and this was disturbing, when those original recordings I wrote got a second life on retrospective Otis Redding albums, somehow my name had disappeared from the writing credits altogether, another bit of industry flim-flammery.

As a result, I have never made a dime on them. Well, let me amend that, I sometimes get a check for maybe fifteen cents. Perhaps they were licensed to other labels by Morey Bernstein because Morey liked to say he had "discovered" Otis Redding, a claim many would make, fully aware that they had not done any such thing. It is not a claim I make. For Morey to make it requires suspending reality. If he discovered him, he sure as hell didn't promote him. Even now, it seems the buzzards are still around trying to feed off Otis; recently, Al Kavelin's son, who runs his late father's estate, contacted me to clarify something about the old copyrights.

My final thought about Otis is that I did what I could for him, and I wish I could have done more. But I could only move on to other projects, looking for the next big thing in music. I rarely even thought of Otis

Redding as our lives pushed on thousands of miles away from each other. The truth was that, back in the day, there were Otis Reddings around each turn. You just had to go find them.

Following through on my plans, a guy named Bruce Chessie and I began a publishing company called Brujem, which we came up with by joining our names. Brujem owned the copyrights for the two released songs by Otis at the time. I wrote a new batch of songs. One was "Christmas Everywhere," which I recorded with Bobby Sheen, the wonderful falsetto singer who Phil Spector used as a backup singer and who performed as the lead singer of Bob B. Soxx and the Blue Jeans, a group that also included Darlene Love and Fanita James. I co-wrote one with Dennis Grillo, "The Sunday School Song," which I believed was a minor classic. I could also produce songs at Gold Star for my own label, Mack IV, a punning reference to Mark VII, Jack Webb's production company (the logo of which closed each episode of *Dragnet*, its imprint created by the thud of a silver hammer) as well as to my family of four: me, Lois, and our two daughters (our son Lyle was still a few years away.) The logo I used was regal looking, a herald from days of old blowing a long coronet. One would never know I ran the company out of my cramped apartment.

I had a few bucks in my pocket by now and people started sending me records. I would buy a song and look for a singer. I cut a lot of demos. I cut one with Sonny Bono, who at the time was trying to break into the business. He had been a waiter, a truck driver, a butcher's helper, before being signed as a staff songwriter at Specialty Records. He wanted me to produce one for him, I cannot recall the name of it, but whatever it was, nothing happened with it and Sonny—with whom I later would act—went on to work with Phil Spector. I was selective in the acts I chose to sign with Mack IV. I had used a trio, Tony Allen, Jimmy Green, and Jerome Evans on lead vocals, to record my demos. Their harmony was superb. I called them the Furys and put them on Mack IV. In '61, I produced their record "Over You" backed with "So Tuff" (I wasn't finished with that theme yet), then a year later, with "Another Fella" and "If There's a Next Time."

Some of the songs were theirs, others mine, and I groomed them to be like the Coasters, an R&B-cum-doo-wop amalgam, with a story line and a lot of personality to each distinctive voice. Tony and Jimmy sang tenor and Jerome's baritone, I'd trade them off on the verses. We sold quite a few records and, again ahead of my time, I put my name on each as the producer—first as "McEachin," then as the storied "Jimmy Mack"—something record labels were loath to do, as some sort of protocol violation. Well, I had followed army and police protocol; my bowing and scraping days were over.

I was getting hotter on the scene. Musical groups beat a path to my apartment at Manhattan Place, but I had trouble keeping those guys in line. Jerome would stab you in the back if he could get a better record deal, and he got a couple. Jimmy wasn't any better. Jimmy would write a song, record it with the Furys in the morning, then in the afternoon sell the same song to another label. I looked up one day and Jimmy had left the Furys and had joined the Medallions with his brother Vernon. They recorded for Dootone and Pan World Records and had some success, opening for Fats Domino at times. Jerome would perform with them, too, or with the Lions, which was a trio I took from Imperial in 1960 that was almost interchangeable with the Furys. With the Lions, I produced "No One," "Giggles," "'Til the 13th of the Month," and "Girl of the World." The Lions were chameleon-like. Their bass singer, James Warren, would rent himself to other groups; he and Jimmy Green were on the Shields' huge hit "You Cheated, You Lied" in 1960. Two other guys sang with the Chimes. Then, more confusingly, in '63 the Lions became the Resonics when they sang "Pepe La Phew."

See, it was all very incestuous, very dog-eat-dog. I still have the teeth marks to prove it because I would be the first one bitten. As the '60s stretched out, the business was changing, unfortunately, for the worse. It was becoming more focused on riches, not talent, not ideas. Decisions were more ironclad. It was less like a family, more like a corporation, and I gave in to that trend. I followed the money. I didn't shutter Mack IV or Brujem, but I was open to freelancing, producing a stray record here and there for a big label, such as Imperial. For two years I had been getting feelers from the labels to come aboard their staffs. Whereas before I thanked them but said no, now I listened.

In '63, Don Blocker, the executive director of Artists and Repertoire at Liberty, called and offered me a job as an A&R man, a very prestigious position. A&R is really just a pretentious way of saying "bird dog," which is what those guys were. The A&R guys would go to clubs and scout talent and songs, a job with tremendous pressure to harvest hit songs and marketable acts, especially at Liberty, which had only been around since 1955, when it was founded as a mainstream pop music label. Its big stars were the chanteuse Julie London, Henry Mancini's orchestra, and the guy who did the Chipmunks songs, Ross Bagdasarian, who called himself David Seville. But they also had great success with the young rock and rollers they pulled out of the L.A. loam, like Billy Ward and the Dominoes, Eddie Cochran, Jan and Dean, and Bobby Vee. They also had Willie Nelson hanging around there, probably smokin' his weed.

In the trade papers, my hiring was news. One bore the headline "Jimmy Mack Joins Liberty A&R Staff." The write-up told of my work and had a nice picture of me pretending to be talking on the phone. "'The addition of Jimmy Mack to our department is most certainly a plus factor in our continuing search for the best in creative talent,' said Blocker. 'His knowledge of the business runs the gamut from R&B to rock n' roll. It is with much excitement that we welcome him to Liberty.'"

I brought the Furys with me to Liberty, and as soon as I arrived there, I was pitched a song that came from the Brill Building stable, written by Carole King and Gerry Goffin, called "Up on the Roof." I thought it was a little corny, a little slow, so I passed on it. I know what you're saying: "McEachin, you fool! How could you say no to that song? Man, it would have made you a million bucks!" Well, it made someone else a million bucks when the Drifters recorded it and sold an astronomical number of records. But every A&R guy who ever worked in the music business has a hundred misses like that. As I did with "These Arms of Mine," you just have to go with your gut. I never looked back at what might have been, because when I looked ahead, there was always something with promise staring me in the face.

Not long after that, another song came to me, "That's Life," written by Dean Kay and Kelly Gordon. Dean ran Lawrence Welk's music publishing company and later became president of Polygram's publishing division, while Kelly would go on to produce Bobbie Gentry's massive hit "Ode to Billy Joe" in 1967. They were a couple of real heavyweights, and "That's Life" was one of those instant hits, expressing the philosophy of getting back up when you're knocked down— "Riding high in April, shot down in May," then "back on top in June." The melody was perfect, the tempo mounting to a slam-bang punch at the end.

Not only was it a great song, but we had the perfect guy to sing it: Gene McDaniels, who came out of the jazz clubs to sign with Liberty. He had a top-ten hit in '61 with "A Hundred Pounds of Clay," sold over a million records, then released a follow-up hit, "Tower of Strength." But Gene always felt the songs they had him sing were bubblegum, that he could be right up there with Frank Sinatra if he could sing serious songs. The problem was that Liberty's roster of artists and producers was almost all white, and they recorded Gene as if he were a white singer. (Later on, he went to Atlantic and recorded very political, race-oriented songs, as well as later writing "Feel Like Making Love" for Roberta Flack.) Gene's regular producer, Snuff Garrett, was a Southern white guy who cut a lot of rockabilly. He was a talent, but I couldn't stand him. I heard that when Gene wanted to quit, someone hung him by his heels outside an upper-floor window until he changed his mind. Knowing the record business as I do, I believe that story. So, when Gene owed Liberty another song, I moved in. I took "That's Life" to him because that song was begging for him to sing it.

Gene loved it, so I moved fast. I went right to the top, Don Blocker, and asked if I could make a demo. Don was noncommittal. He said I should go to Al Bennett, Liberty's then-vice president (who David Seville had named Alvin the Chipmunk after, and the other two Chipmunks after other Liberty honchos). Bennett was the guy at the top of the chain in picking the songs, so I went to him. "How perfect is this song for Gene?" I asked, and told him I wanted to make a demo, which would have cost maybe three hundred bucks—no skin off Liberty's backside. Al listened to half the song, then shook his head.

"No. I don't like it. Don't make a demo."

Well, I couldn't accept that. I knew he was dead wrong. So, I decided the hell with it: I'd record it with Gene anyway. I thought once Al heard Gene singing it, he'd flip. I set up a session with Gene at the NBC Studio, where they had the latest state-of-the-art equipment. Gene Page arranged it. The musicians were on point and Gene knocked it out of the park. He never sang better. I walked out afterward that night thinking we had a smash. Dubbing it down the next day, I was all smiles.

Liberty had a big staff meeting on Wednesday mornings, when everyone—executives, producers, writers, A&R guys—would all gather in

Al's office and listen to the latest demos, then vote on which ones to release. Snuff Garrett played his Bobby Vee stuff, Dick Glasser played his, then the others. I was the last guy, the new kid in town, the low man on the totem pole. The black guy. I put my record on. When Al realized it was "That's Life," he looked at me as if I were public enemy number one. He was angry, so angry that he scared me. Veins were popping all over his head. Without even listening to it, he ripped into me for having disobeyed his judgment and making a record billed to Liberty without authorization.

"Get that piece of crap out of here! We're not going to release a ghetto song!" he bellowed. "And you get outta here. You're fired!"

I can only assume it was because a black man in the kingdom had the temerity to undercut his authority. I don't think Snuff Garrett would have ever gotten a tongue-lashing like that. I didn't have to put up with that treatment from anyone: I didn't check my principles at the door when I came to Liberty. I couldn't have cared less because I wasn't a company man. I was my own man. I had proven that more than a few times.

I didn't try to change Al's mind. I didn't kill him with a thumb to the eyeball, which I could have done. I was a bigger man than him. I simply took the disk off the record player, left his office, and marched down the hallway to begin cleaning out my desk, shaking my head at the myopia of a man who would fire someone for giving him a sure-fire hit, just because his pride was singed. Then, before walking out the door for the last time, I put the record on my player and blasted it as loud as it could go. You could have heard it on Sunset Boulevard. It resounded through the corridors of Liberty, making the walls shake. I said to myself, If I'm fired, y'all are gonna know why!

Suddenly, a guy rushed into my office. I recognized him as Jimmy Bowen, who was producing Frank Sinatra, Dean Martin, and Sammy Davis, Jr., at Sinatra-owned Reprise Records. "Jimmy, that's a hell of a tune," he said.

"Yeah, tell those turkeys down there."

He asked if he could buy the record. I said, "Buy it? Jimmy, I am out of here. You can have it."

A little shocked, he took it, said, "Thank you," and flew out of the office, looking like he had found a bag on the floor holding a million dollars. And you know something—he had.

"That's Life" was actually recorded twice before Jimmy produced it with Frank Sinatra in 1966, using Gene McDaniels' performance and Gene Page's arrangement as the blueprint. With Reprise, the song lived up to the potential I saw in it for Gene; Frank's version hit number one on the chart and became the title track of his latest album. The song made a fortune for Reprise, boosting the bottom line for Warner Brothers' showbiz mega-corporation, its parent company.

Al Bennett's woefully bad decision, meanwhile, didn't help Liberty's bottom line any. Other bad decisions were already sinking the company in a morass of red ink; in 1964, it would be sold to Avnet, an electronics firm that owned a record label, for $12 million. Liberty remained active and Al became its president. Then, two years later, Avnet was sold for $8 million—to Al Bennett. Al did all right for himself, and so did Liberty, which continued to be a giant in the industry into the 1990s—when its president, in a round- about irony, was none other than Jimmy Bowen.

My tenure at Liberty lasted all of two weeks. But I left with something more important than money: my convictions and self-pride, as well as Mack IV and Brujem. We always had work, not only from people in the music industry, but from advertising agencies as well. They commissioned us to write the music for big ad campaigns, and not just jingles but entire scripts for commercials. I still have the typewritten scripts for Mr. Clean, Starkist Tuna, and Newport cigarettes. Some were done in the manner of a rhythmic rap, with cool bass lines. One for Starkist began:

"This is a story about the time all the TV commercials

Got together over at the little Winemaker's pad.

But Charlie Tuna thought he'd been had

And he bounced around the room quite disturbed

'Cause there was no refreshments being served. "

It went from there into a whole story, the novelty of it being that it never mentioned tuna. The Furys, who I had taken back from Liberty, recorded some of the tracks, as Jerome had a voice for that sort of thing. We were thinking out of the box, and I still think those would have been classic commercials. But the sponsors didn't follow up with us, making it a waste of time, which I hated then and still do. I needed to be moving ahead, like a shark. And I was still quite busy. I had the Furys cut a whole bunch of songs before the group began to fall apart, the biggest being "What is Soul" and an updated rock/soul version of the old showtune "Zing! Went the Strings of My Heart." Also, times were changing. I did a lot of those songs trying to turn the Furys into another Flamingos or Drifters. I did one-off sessions for Specialty, World Pacific, and Infinity. I did some jazz sessions with Les McCann. I did some demos with Eartha Kitt.

I had so much on my plate that I hired H. B. Barnum (of Little Rascals fame) to produce some records for me—an important break for H. B., who had sung with the Dootones and the Robins before moving into arranging and production. He later produced everyone from Sinatra to Aretha Franklin to Gladys Knight. Then I signed a guy named Alexander Patton, who had a gruffly resonant voice in the mode of James Brown and David Ruffin, more soulful than Otis Redding's, and I mean that. He had done a couple of records for the Duo-Disc label and then was signed by Capitol and came to me to produce his first song. We had a writer, Lee Brackett, who wanted to be a singer but was a better songwriter, and he wrote "A Lil Lovin' Sometimes." I produced it at Capitol's studio in 1965 with Motown-style horns, a hard-driving four-four drumbeat, slap bass, and female background singers. I tried to put a little bit of every great soul singer in it—any of whom could have sung it—and Alexander came through. The song sounded like a chugging train, a supersonic train, and Alexander just crushed it. Why he didn't make it big in the music business, I don't know, given the way he killed it singing, "Everybody needs, everybody wants, everybody got to have true lovin' sometimes."

These little gems usually made it on to the R&B charts, and they were rewarding achievements; many would be recognized decades later by soul music historians as pivotal to the genre. As a result, through the years people have inquired about buying the Mack IV song catalog (sans "She's All Right," which was stolen from me), but

I didn't want to bother with the legalisms and the paperwork. Then, too, the Beatles had changed everything around, turned the business upside down. Even though the British musicians had been influenced by American rockers, like Little Richard and Chuck Berry—and my own reputation was bigger in England than in the States—the old standards were becoming anachronistic. Groups were writing their own songs, playing their own instruments.

It didn't faze me at the time. I had such an easy time in the music business, and I hadn't known anything when I started! I was very naive. I felt that I could have gone on with it. I would meet people, big stars, just as a matter of course. When I wanted someone to distribute the Furys records, I spoke with Fred Astaire's music publisher, Steve Topley, who introduced me to Fred. Life was like that, a carousel of wonder. But things change, the carousel turns. I didn't appreciate the snakes running the business or the petty games they played. My partner Bruce would quit the business about two years later to play jazz, going back to his roots. And me, I sensed I might have another calling, though what that was I didn't yet know.

And then, just like that, I got a ticket out, because of something that could have only been predestined given how unlikely it was. One day, walking down Melrose Avenue, diagonally across the street from Paramount Studios, a guy bumped into me and looked me over.

"Aint'chu an actor?"

"No."

"Wanna be one?"

"Don't know why I should be."

"Follow me."

Well, I thought the guy was gay, and I wasn't interested—but not for long. His name was Art Names, and he had written a movie called *I Crossed the Color Line.* "Upstairs, right through that door," he said, pointing.

That's a story for the next chapter. But I'll end with one last footnote to my time as Jimmy Mack, music man. Years later, when I was an established actor, I was in a bar and a guy walked in, saw me, and came over. It was Don Blocker.

"You son of a bitch!" he said. "I made you famous!"

"Really? How did you make me famous?"

"Remember Liberty Records? Remember 'That's Life'? If we hadn't fired you, we would have released that goddamn song!"

"Don, if you had done that, I would still be in the music business."

"Jimmy, you should thank me for that. I got you a new career as a movie star!"

Jimmy Mack Joins Liberty A&R Staff

HOLLYWOOD—Don Blocker, executive A & R director of Liberty Records, has signed Jimmy ("Mack") McEachin to an exclusive contract as an a & r producer for the label.

Mack, who will headquarter at the label's Hollywood offices, plans to develop his own artists in addition to taking on several Liberty contractees. He has already pacted The Furys quartet to a term pact and plans immediate sessions.

With a musical background which includes promotion as well as production, Mack's previous associations include Infinity Records as a producer, and following the death of Infinity's owner, Cliff Garrett, the World Pacific label.

"The addition of Jimmy Mack to our department is most certainly a plus factor in our continuing search for the best in creative talent," said Blocker. "His knowledge of the business runs the gamut from r & b to rock n' roll. It is with much excitement that we welcome him to Liberty."

CHAPTER 6

THE SILVER (AND BLACK) SCREEN

I did not walk through the door across the street, as Art Names suggested. I was just about to walk away from him. But Art was so enthusiastic, he kept on extolling the script he had written, which intrigued me a bit because Art was an unprepossessing white man who was the classic Hollywood hustler. He had no credits to his name but did have inordinate ambition to film *I Crossed the Color Line*, the plot of which had to do with a black man taking revenge on the Ku Klux Klan for killing his daughter. One has to remember, this was 1965, and it was rare for Hollywood to become heavily invested in those sorts of storylines, lest white audiences get too scared of uppity black men.

Even in the record business, black artists usually labored for slave-wage royalty arrangements. Not until the '70s were even top-selling black artists judged mainstream enough to be considered for Grammys in anything but R&B and jazz categories. By 1965, only two black actors had been recognized with an Oscar: Hattie McDaniel had won one for her infamous stereotypical supporting role as a black maid, Mammy, in *Gone with the Wind*, and my good friend Sidney Poitier won best actor in 1963 for *Lilies of the Field*. It would be another nineteen years before Lou Gossett won for his role in *An Officer and a Gentleman*. To this day, only fourteen black actors have been awarded one of those statuettes.

So, the lilies weren't exactly ripe for a movie like *I Crossed the Color Line*, not at the time when reruns of *Amos 'n' Andy* were still being seen on TV. Most movie fare with racial themes was on the order of *Lilies of the Field* and the movie adaptation of the Broadway play *Purlie Victorious* the same year starring Ossie Davis and Ruby Dee. Both were uplifting fables in which idealistic black men ingratiate themselves to whites in Jim Crow times; Sidney was even taken as a saint sent by God. A more intense picture, *Black Like Me*, had a rather good actor, James Whitmore, assuming the identity of a black man to experience racism in the Deep South. That was daring for the era, but Art's script was far out: a light-skinned black man infiltrates the Klan, whereupon all hell breaks loose. That was fairly radical in the mid-60s, and it did intrigue me. At the very least, I wanted to know more about the project and this thing called acting.

In my naivete, I didn't reckon it would take much to act; I figured I'd just say some lines, get paid, and go home. The fact that I didn't hightail it down the street was proof to Art that I was coming around. He suggested that I meet the producer of the film, whose office was in a building nearby.

I still wasn't quite ready for that, so he said, "Let's have some lunch." He probably knew that would hook me—a free meal was always welcome. We proceeded to a nearby restaurant, and he further explained the plot of the movie, which was so convoluted I could barely understand it. Then he dragged me upstairs to meet the producer Joe Solomon and the director Ted V. Mikels.

Talk about a character! Though I had never heard of Ted Mikels, and he hadn't done much in the business, with his waxed, foot-long mustache, beret, and ascot, he looked like Cecil B. DeMille. I would learn that he lived in a big house in Glendale that looked like a castle where he held wild parties. I was told a lot of crazy stuff went on there, though I didn't want to know exactly what. I also learned he had his own studio, producing low-budget B-movies with no-name actors and titles like *Dr. Sex* and *Orgy of the Dead*. He owned a small record label, as well. Clearly, a little could go a long way in Hollywood back then—if you looked the part.

In reality, this was the lowest rung of the business, the underbelly. But it didn't matter a bit to me since I knew nothing about the movie business. I was just amazed that an hour earlier I had been walking down the street, and now I was going to be an actor without remotely knowing what that entailed. All Ted needed was to see me. "Art," he declared, "this is the guy!"

Later, it would all become a little clearer to me. It seemed all they wanted to do was keep the shooting schedule on time, because time was money, and the company didn't have a whole lot of it. Art was basically on the street looking to hire the first black guy he came upon. And they were thrilled that I was a music man, because the part was that of a musician. "He's perfect!" Art told Ted. Then I met the executive producer, Joe Solomon, another character. He filled my head with hyperbole such as, "We got a great movie here, and it'll be because of you!" What's more, just being myself made them even more sure about me. Ted said I should read from the script for them. Well, I didn't want to do that because I'd never seen a script before. And I still wasn't sold on doing this acting thing, and I tried to get that point across.

"Can't you see I'm not interested in acting?" I said, with some exasperation.

But all that did was make them think I was, in fact, an actor and so confident that I didn't need to read. It seemed I couldn't do anything wrong.

"Well, at least take the script home, read it, see what you think," Ted urged, almost pleading. "Get back to me by tomorrow."

I agreed to do at least that much. They were going to be shooting in a couple of days in Bakersfield, California, so they were in a hurry. But I wasn't. I threw the script into the trunk of my car and didn't think anything more about it. A couple of days later, I got a call from Ted's office., "Are you Jimmy Mack? You were supposed to be here for an audition."

I had forgotten completely about it. "Oh yeah, yeah," I fibbed.

"Well, are you going to do it or not? You want the role or not?" I kind of stammered around and he said, "Well, if you want it— it's yours. We're paying four hundred dollars. That good enough for you?"

And at that point, needing money as I always did, and not currently having a job, it was.

"Yeah, yeah," I said. "Of course!"

He gave me directions to the set in Bakersfield and the schedule for shooting the next day. I guess that minute on the phone was my audition.

A little later that day, I got another call, this one from Max Julien, a black actor who was also in the movie. Great guy, too. He was young, maybe twenty, and this was his first film after doing stage work off-Broadway in New York. Wherein I knew absolutely nothing about the stage or anything about show-business, except for my relatively brief stint in the record business, Max was the real deal as an actor and would subsequently perform in both TV and movies (one of which, I might note, was *The Mack*, from which some of his lines would be sampled on rap records). He dated and lived with Vonetta McGee, a wonderful actress who I would later recommend for a part in a Clint Eastwood movie. But back then, I didn't know him, nor he me.

"I understand you're gonna be in our movie?" he said.

"I guess so."

"Well, good. You got a car? I'll ride up there with you."

Keep in mind, I hadn't even read the script—I had never even seen a script before, and I had no idea what I was supposed to do. I made arrangements with Max, and the next morning at 7:00 a.m., I picked him up on the corner down from the restaurant. He explained on the ride to the location address in Bakersfield what the part was. Max needed this role, and so he was very invested in my being acceptable. He was coaching and giving me motivation for the part, which was still a mystery to me. All I knew was that I was playing a musician, which was no great stretch, of course. But Max almost died at my nonchalance. "You mean, you don't know the lines?"

"No, and I don't want to know."

Max stuck close to me, showing me the ropes, and I'm glad he did, because when we got there and the other actors started showing up, I was taken aback. The white actors playing the Klan members looked like escapees from a chain gang. Then we filmed a scene—which was a black man being hanged. Welcome to acting.

My role was that of friend to the black man whose daughter had been killed by the Klan. His character went to Alabama to kill the guys who did it, and my character would rescue him. That was the scene we rehearsed first, and it didn't go well. The acting was sloppy, nobody was happy, and all I was thinking was, how can I get the hell outta here? They tried to instruct me on where to stand and all that, but it was so confusing I just stood back and watched. I was to drive a car into the hanging scene, so I did. But nobody told me I was supposed to stop short before I got out. So, I just kept going, knocking over equipment, and sending people scattering for their lives. Ted, who gave directions through a megaphone, yelled, "Goddammit! What the hell are you doin'?"

It got more preposterous. The producers hadn't told the authorities in Bakersfield that they were doing a movie, didn't get a permit or anything. And during the shoot, a state trooper who was driving by looked down into the ravine where we were shooting and saw a bonfire, which was part of the scene because the Klan hoods were made of satin and the fire reflecting off them created an eerie effect. The trooper thought a real hanging was going on. He tore down into the ravine and yelled, "Halt! What's going on here?" Then, reaching for his gun, he commanded, "Take off those hoods!"—and, to his great shock, every one of the guys under those damn hoods was black, because they were extras being used in the scene. The trooper damn near had a heart attack, but it got Ted off the hook, and we muddled through the rest of the movie before the budget ran out.

It was a comedy of errors. An extra, some guy named Leroy, stole one of the cameras. The police who were investigating the theft went by Leroy's house, and he had this enormous, bulky camera sitting there in his living room. His explanation was, "If it don't move, steal it," which might be the creed of more than a few movie people. I just smiled at the ludicrousness of the whole thing. I ended up getting my close-ups, didn't have to say much in the way of lines, and that was that: four bills in the bank. Somehow, all involved survived the shoot and went on to bigger and better things. It was the worst movie ever made, and Ted the most inept director I've ever known. His intention was good, but it went very, very badly. I can say without reservation that I was the worst thing in the worst movie ever made. The good thing was, I had used the name Jimmy Mack for it. That name was killed forever.

Months later, I was so embarrassed when I went to the premiere of, *I Crossed the Color Line* at a theater on the Sunset Strip that I wouldn't even take Lois to it. Not being a show-biz aficionado, she wouldn't have gone anyway, but I did give Max a ride. Ted got up and made a big speech, saying, "This movie is one of the most important productions ever," and really he believed it. In the theater that night, the audience sat there in stunned silence, except for Max, that is. During a closeup, or when his name came up in the credits, he would erupt, cheering and applauding himself.

Me? Before it was over, I had snuck out.

The producer Joe Solomon published ads that crowed about the movie making $81,610 at the Paramount Theater in Newark and $48,102 at twelve drive-ins around San Francisco; there were also images of the lead actress and actor, alongside the heavy-breathing copy: "This is Andrea . . . She had to have his love . . . even though her baby might be BLACK!" and "This is Jerry ... He passed for white . . . to please the innermost secrets of the white man . . . and his women!" It did no good. Few came to see the movie and it soon disappeared. And yet the movie—the title of which was changed to the more emphatic *The Black Klansman*—would survive in some circles as one of those unintentionally funny cult classics.

Amazingly enough, I found that, for myself, it was more than a four-hundred-dollar lark. For one thing, Ted loved me. He would tell me for years after, "Jimmy, I made you a star!" I ended up being the biggest name he ever worked with! And in Hollywood, it's not how great or rich you are, or how good or bad the movies you make are. It's simply that you have something, some "it" factor, that translates to the screen. (And if you come cheap, even better.) Apparently, on the basis of a few scenes in a dud, industry types concluded I had that undefinable "it." And so launched my career on the silver screen.

None of this is to suggest that I had any delusions that I was a real actor, but it seemed the movie crowd in L.A. did. Soon after that debacle, and I swear this is true, I was walking on the same street where Art had first run across me, and a guy named Alon Cory was walking the other way and recognized me. Apparently, he was one of the handful of people who saw the movie. He stopped, introduced himself as an agent, and said, "You know, I think I can get you some parts." Alon, who had been a small-time actor in the '50s, already had a project lined up. MGM was doing a picture with producer and director Robert Aldrich called *The Legend of Lylah Clare*. Aldrich was a real heavy hitter, having already made the groundbreaking film *What Ever Happened to Baby Jane?* and he would go on to later direct the great war movie *The Dirty Dozen*. *Lylah Clare*, which had been a TV drama, was a big-budget item, costing around $3.5 million to make. A social parable about the sins and venality of Hollywood, it starred the sultry Kim Novak in a dual role as an actress hired to portray a long-ago murdered actress, Kim playing both roles.

And, just like that, Alon called me and said, "I got you an interview over at MGM. It's not much of a role, but all you've got to do is go there and tell 'em I sent you." So, I did, and the assistant looked me up and down and said, "You're fine. You got the role."

I called Al with the news, he said, "They already called me. You got it. It's a one-day job."

"What're they paying?" I asked.

"A thousand," he said.

I exclaimed, "What?" Whoever thought movies would be this easy? I had no lines, and the scene I would be in was going to be shot the next day. All I knew was I would be playing a TV reporter in a crowd of other reporters peppering Lylah with questions. When I got to the set, Aldrich told me where to stand and to wave my arms around and such. And that was it. I was done, a thousand dollars heavier in the wallet.

I thought, I'm gonna get a thousand dollars for that? Are you kidding me?

Indeed, for a guy appearing in one scene, people seemed to take notice of me. Peter Finch, the British actor who was the co-star, playing a tortured director who had been married to Lylah, started talking to me quite cordially. Later, I learned why. He was living with a black woman, and he seemed to feel he needed to overcompensate, to show his affinity for black people. When he saw me, he wanted me to be his black friend. At the wrap party, held at MGM, he got inebriated and gave a slurring declaration about how he loved a black woman and didn't care who knew it. The truth was, nobody cared who the hell he was sleeping with, least of all me, because, and I'll add this cautiously, I had my eye on very sultry Miss Novak. I thought she might have had her eye on me, but I was respectful of her and everyone else on the set. It was still a whirlwind to me. My head was spinning in this new reality, so I just minded my p's and q's, which might have been why Aldrich, who didn't know me from Adam, told me he might have more work for me.

There must have been some reason why I kept moving upward, because I didn't appear, nor should I have, in the credits of the movie. When it hit finally the theaters in November 1968, it was tarred and feathered by the critics as melodramatic hamming and was a bomb at the box office. I barely took note of it, because Alon had gotten me bit parts in other big-budget movies the same year. It was nothing to brag about. But under the radar, I had begun making some inroads on my own. I had walked in the right door at the right time, and I liked the lifestyle of the actors and producers I was meeting. It turned my head a bit. Using my connection with MGM, such as it was, I was permitted to hang around on the lot, which was an opportunity to keep myself in the loop, rub elbows with people, be seen. Alon sent out a flurry of letters to casting directors, pitching me as "an actor whom I think merits your attention" or "a brilliant negro actor," along with an eight-by-ten photo of my mug.

It didn't take long for the MGM connection to pay off. The studio was making a light comedy about the 1965 New York blackout, *Where Were You When the Lights Went Out?* starring Doris Day. When Alon called and told me, "Hey, get right down there, they're making a Doris

Day movie," you could have knocked me over with a feather. Doris Day! That was big!

They were shooting on the same sound stage as *Lylah Clare* had. The director, Hy Averback, had mainly done television comedies and fluff, which was what the movie was. For the same pay, a thousand bucks, but no credit, all I had to do was direct traffic in a studio set made to look like Grand Central Station. I was in good company—do you know who else was an uncredited extra in the movie? None other than Morgan Freeman.

I did get something vital out of the gig, however, by being able to observe Doris acting. She was a wonderful, very underrated actress, and watching her do a scene, the ease with which she animated sterile lines on a page, was highly educational to me. What's more, she was a genuinely nice lady, unlike the leading man, Patrick O'Neal, who working with again later did nothing to sway my opinion that he was vain and supercilious.

I had become one of the boys at MGM—the guy with no credits and no idea of how to act. I never had to wait long for another role to come up. I had just finished the movie when Alon called about a TV show being produced by another studio starring Chuck Connors of *Rifleman* fame. There was a paucity of black actors in TV at the time. That was about to change, and I got in on the cusp when Chuck Connors did a series produced by Ivan Tors, who had produced the top-rated *Sea Hunt* series for many years, filming most scenes underwater. Now, he had developed one called *Cowboy in Africa*, with Chuck playing an American rancher and horse breeder who relocates to Africa to show the natives about modern ranch techniques. It sounded rather pedestrian, but Chuck loved outdoorsy, physical roles that didn't typecast him as a gunslinger. I got to know him and, as rugged as he was, he had more refined tastes than anyone knew.

The short-lived series was shot in L.A., out in rustic Antelope Valley, and they needed an actor to play a Kenyan doctor, Dr. Lee Matsis, in an episode titled "Stone Age Safari." They wanted "an authentic African," and I really wanted the role, so I called the UCLA African Studies Center and spoke with a couple of people there who taught me some African phrases. When I arrived at the Ivan Tors

Studio, I stood at the front desk, repeating those phrases to the receptionist. She had no idea what I was saying and went inside. A minute later, Ivan Tors himself came out and excitedly ushered me in. He realized I was there for the role and with me still muttering unintelligible gibberish. His eyes widened with delight, "Oh boy," he said to some of his associates, one being co-creator Andy White, "we have a real African here."

He had on his desk one of those snow-globe things. I sat down and reached for it, looking fascinated with the snow, continuing my muttering. I must say, it was perhaps my finest acting role. When he asked me, in halting English, about my background, I replied in my own imperfect English and pseudo-African that I was an "an-throo-pol-ee-gist."

"Great," he said. "Because you will play a 'doctah.'" It was all I could do not to break out in a gust of laughter. I was thinking, Wow! He believes I am really an African doctor! Ivan and his people were high fiving each other, figuring they had found the perfect guy for the role. He had me read from the script, which I did using the same fake dialect. Ivan was pleased. "You, sir," he said, extending his hand, "have got yourself a job."

Mind you, I had no résumé or anything, and he didn't want one. Nor did he care that when I filled out the working papers, the name James McEachin was not exactly a typical African. All he knew was he had the guy he wanted for the role. I asked, "Where you shoot movie?" Once I had the directions, I got out of there as quickly as I could, barely keeping a straight face. And that is how the role of an authentic African doctor went to an authentic New Jerseyan known as Jimmy Mack. More than that, the show called Al and said they loved me so much, they were giving me twice the money, which was, I believe, twenty-five hundred dollars.

I was on cloud nine, but the script had a lot of lines for me. I walked around the studio trying to memorize them. There was a glitch when the producers called Al and said they found out I wasn't a member of the Screen Actors Guild, which was a requirement for the job. They were all pissed off at Alon for misleading them about me being an actor as well as a doctor. Quick-thinking Alon told them, "Of course he's not in the American Screen Actors Guild, you idiots—he works in Africa!"

And it worked. They let up on it and I got right over to SAG, where Al paid my membership fee. All was in order. I learned the lines, did my fake African accent, and got my check. Chuck and I became friends. The thing about Chuck was, he longed to be taken seriously as an actor. He hated the *Rifleman* image and walked around quoting Shakespeare if you can believe Lucas McCain as King Lear. I saw him in a much more human way; he was so big and, yet, so insecure. I kept reassuring him that he was going to win an Emmy. He never did, and the show was canceled after one season. Still, after I had filmed my episode, I received a letter from Chuck, a letter I still have and have kept in pristine condition. It reads:

Dear James,

Just a note to say thank you for your contribution to our *Cowboy in Africa* series segment entitled "Stone Age Safari.' I enjoyed working with you. Sincerely,

Chuck

Clearly, I had bigger, tastier fish to fry in acting than in music. I never did close Mack IV Records and Brujem Publishing—which are still technically in business—but I bid adieu to the artists I was producing. The Furys had just about had it, anyway, each going in a different direction. Just try dealing with all those creeps in the industry or managing four guys who had no discipline. I was more excited about acting and running in the Hollywood bullring with stars. My acting method was to just believe the character and project his personality, calmly, without hamming it up. I believed whatever appeal I had was directly linked to my ability to seem natural, as if not acting at all. The "it" I had, I wanted to keep. That was why even though I always had trouble memorizing lines, I could fudge it by improvising if I had to, which could make the dialogue better, more real. Never mind the real reason was I had no idea what the next line was.

This was an approach that worked particularly well on the stage. In November '67, I dipped my toes in the theater for the first time, getting a part in *Day of Absence*. This was the second of two one-act satires by Douglas Turner Ward being staged in a limited run at the Ebony Showcase Theater in L.A. In 1966 the show had won a Vernon Rice Drama Desk Award for best off-Broadway play of the season. The material was scathing. *Day of Absence* was set in an imaginary Southern town where all the black people had simply vanished, save for the ones left sick and dying in a hospital. To the shock of the whites, life without black people was no picnic, there being no one to shine their shoes and no criminals to keep the police occupied, prompting the racist mayor to beg, "Erase this nightmare 'n' we'll concede any demand you make, just come on back—please?"

The black actors, identified as "crackers," wore whiteface—the lone white actor did the same, without the need for makeup, narrating the proceedings—which bore a similarity to the black actors playing Klansmen in *I Crossed the Color Line*. But this time there was nothing to snicker at. The nuance was right up my alley, requiring both high and restrained emotion and a twinkle in the eye—my natural predilections—in the role of a town layabout. A lingering memory, as well, is that the best actor on the stage was Isabel Sanford, who spelled her name "Isabell" then, as a rich white doyen who wakes up horrified that her black maid isn't around any longer (again, with some irony, as Isabel would soon be playing a black doyen on *The Jeffersons*). She rightly received most of the glowing reviews, but my work did not go unnoticed. *The Los Angeles Times* critic wrote, "Jim McEachin and Jai Rich are hilarious as two stereotyped and painted white 'crackers' who philosophize on the importance of the event."

A postscript is that the play was performed annually for years at Evergreen State College in Olympia, Washington, and revived on Broadway in 2018—but it also created controversy in these highly sensitive times, and Evergreen canceled it in 2017 when threatened with a lawsuit claiming the white-faced characterizations displayed "hostility based on race." This was patently absurd, showing a gross ignorance of the motives of a great playwright. I am grateful for having been a part of it. As far as I'm concerned, the play was exceptional and an invaluable step in my evolution as an actor.

More important than any acting method, however, was the art of auditioning. Here's my rule: If you have personality, you can ace it. Be normal, be inventive, say what you think you can bring to the character. I was incredibly lucky. Alon just kept lining up parts. I'd go to the auditions, where I was becoming a somewhat familiar face, and I would get the jobs. That happened with my second movie that would hit the screens in 1968, *Coogan's Bluff*, which Clint Eastwood made under the aegis of the company he had begun with *Hang 'Em High*, The Malpaso Company. Eastwood began the company with an accountant named Irving Leonard, the objective being to run a tight ship and keep budgets in line.

Coogan's Bluff was distributed by Universal, earned Clint a million dollars, and took him out of his "man with no name" roles in the Sergio Leone "spaghetti westerns." I admit I had never seen him in any movie or in his first starring role, on the cowboy TV series *Rawhide*. I generally ignored westerns, those little morality plays built around strong, silent—and always white—heroes who killed scores of bad guys while never getting a nick or a scratch. This movie, though, put him in a different role, that of an Arizona deputy sheriff who travels to New York to extradite a fugitive killer. Don Siegel was the director, and he would go on to make a total of five movies with Clint—three with me in them.

It came about because I had made myself familiar with the Universal studio, which was not too far from where I lived. I had heard it was like a college campus, with a lot of parties going on, and I wanted in, so I made it my business to befriend as many of the Universal casting directors as I could, including my favorite, Don McElwaine. There was also Tom Jennings, Bob LaSanka, and the very thankless Rueben Cannon. If I got an audition, I got the job probably ninety-eight percent of the time. Letting me into the same building with the casting directors was like letting the fox in the coop with the chickens. Long before my all-fields contract with Universal, I would be in the office, eyeballing the other black actors auditioning for the same part. I could usually wangle the script before I got there through connections, so when a secretary would ask if I wanted the script, I would say, "No, thank you. I already read it." At that, the other actors would get irate, thinking I had been given special treatment; to my delight, they'd get up and leave, and some were far better actors than me.

Most remarkably, I found out later that Don Siegel, without even knowing much about me, had actually wanted me to do a big part *in Coogan's Bluff*, not the small one I tried out for, that of a prisoner being released from jail in the police station, for which I would have maybe one or two words of dialogue. It seemed that Don Stroud, one of the co-stars, was a troublemaker. He showed up late and argued a lot, testing Siegel's and Clint's patience. Apparently, Siegel was going to fire Stroud and put me in his role as the fugitive killer. But they got him in line, and I got the small part with no audition. Although I made the credits only as "man," I didn't really care. It was the face time that counted, no matter how little.

Funny how these things work in Hollywood. I didn't do much in the movie. I said almost nothing to Clint, not wanting to disturb him, though he seemed to be respectful of all the actors, and I could see why he had become a big star; he was ruggedly and roguishly handsome, his hair all windswept and falling over his eyes, and he had that low-key magnetism and sledgehammer intensity that defined the antihero, which was the beau idéal of all actors. I also spent a lot of time studying Lee J. Cobb, the rubber-faced veteran actor who was the other co-star; his intensity was more up my alley, not overshadowing the star, yet holding his own in any scene. But the real dividend of being in a major movie was that I became known by name at Universal, and I used that recognition as a means to an end.

I noticed that there was a strange sort of herd mentality among the executives. Every day at noon, like clockwork, all the executives, (dressed nearly identically in dark suits), would come down at the same time for their three-martini lunch. It was like the song "Baby Elephant Walk" was playing as they moved along in lockstep. One day, in the lobby by the elevators, I waited and watched, wanting to pick out the most important-looking guy. I finally spotted him.

"Tell me something," I said. "How the hell does a guy get any work around here?"

The guy looked at me, puzzlement in his eyes. "What do you do?"

"Well, I'm a writer, and I'm looking for a place here to work."

"Okay, call my office after lunch," he said, handing me his card. It read Norman Glenn. "We'll see what we can do."

Around three o'clock that afternoon, I called Mr. Norman Glenn and turned on the charm.

"Hey, Mr. Glenn, how's it going, my friend? Listen, remember in the lobby, you said to call you?"

"Oh, yes. So, what are you writing?"

"Well, I've got a couple of scripts here that I want to get on paper." Then, without pausing for breath: "A corner office would do just fine."

I admit, it took some brass stones to do that. Being direct, not tiptoeing around on eggshells, is often the only way to get the impossible done. And it worked.

"Oh, sure," he said. "Give me a few minutes to make a call."

Sure enough, when I called back, my new best friend Norman said, "We have some places open, I have just the right kind of space for you."

So not only did I get an office, I got to pick the office. It was in a little hotel across the street from the lot, and it remained that way until Universal changed it into offices and later into a post office. It was perfect. It had a little refrigerator, shower, desk, phone—everything I needed.

"I think," I said coyly, "this just might work."

The head of housing for Universal, a guy named Jim, even helped me lay out the office and fix it up real nice. Here I was, a bit-part actor whose only credit was "man," and I was all set up at Universal Studios. I was even given a seven-year contract as a scriptwriter. I think they paid me three hundred dollars a week. Just as valuable, my name was on the door. I would call up people, old friends, and exclaim, "Hey, I'm in my new office at Universal!" That would leave them with their jaws agape. I was within the studio culture. John Cassavetes had an office over there; in addition to his acting work, he wrote the verité-style movie *Faces*, which he directed, and which starred his wife, Gena Rowlands. That movie won him an Oscar nomination for best original screenplay in '69.

Steven Spielberg, also hustling in the background at the studio, was an unpaid gofer on the movie, and we hung out at the new place. We had our little coterie. Steven Bochco was another in the crowd. He was a young guy and had just graduated with a theater degree. He had an office near mine from where he would develop and write scripts for a gaggle of hit Universal TV series, like *The Bold Ones: The New Doctors, The Invisible Man, McMillan & Wife,* and *Columbo,* before he hit the jackpot with *Hill Street Blues,* which starred his wife, Barbara Bosson. We became friends, and some of his shows would be a lifeline for me, which was more than a little helpful since the studio wanted me to come up with ideas for movies and, unlike Steven, I didn't have any, nor any scripts to work on. A mere technicality.

The crazy thing was, nobody really knew what my job was at Universal, but they knew my face and my name. Admittedly, I had come around at the right time, when Hollywood belatedly started opening up to black men as if to compensate for the industry's history of racial exclusion. They wanted to have a tight-knit circle of black actors they knew, and so I became part of a network of powerful people—people I could not believe I knew. In time, I would walk down the hall and there would be Sid Sheinberg, president of Universal TV—which really was the backbone of the company, as its movie division was not yet a big money-maker. Steven Spielberg had been working on Sid, too, and he knew the game. In '68, after Steven, who was only twenty-one at the time, had directed his first film, a short movie called *Amblin,* Sid, who himself was only in his thirties, hired him to a seven-year contract— at the bargain-basement price of three hundred a week. Like me, Steven didn't care about money; he wanted to ride the up escalator. He directed a segment in the pilot episode of the Night Gallery series and did some other minor work on other shows, but he was biding time. I knew all about that waiting game.

It was just normal for me to receive a call to get myself over to the set and fill a role in a movie or TV show, or even a theater gig. It got so that I didn't need Alon to pitch me. In fact, I began to realize that Alon had been using me as leverage to get to Don and Guy McElwaine and Bob LaSanka and Tom Jennings. I found that off-putting. As it was, Alon was taking his commission plus deducting a percentage for the SAG members' pension plan from my payment. He also wasn't representing any high rollers; his roster of talent was middling. And so, in the fall of '67, I wrote Alon that I was "exercising my right to terminate both of my Television and Theatrical Motion Picture Artists' Contracts," signing the missive, "With all good wishes, James McEachin." It may have been perfunctory, but I never was good at sugar coating.

I did not hire another agent. I didn't even want to have my good friend Don McElwaine represent me. It meant something to me to go it alone. And, again, the timing was right. What with my place at Universal and its reach in TV—in the late '60s and well beyond, their shows accounted for more hours on the tube than all other studios combined—my "reliability" as a black actor naturally became a sinecure. I braced myself, knowing the next few years would be hectic and probably more than a bit stomach churning.

Tragically, Don McElwaine, the one who did a great deal of nursing my career along, passed away at just forty-six. He never got the chance to see just how fruitful my stay at Universal could be. His brother, Guy, was a high-powered agent and later became president of Columbia Pictures during the *Ghostbusters* and *Gandhi* days. I got to know Guy well, too. Whenever I'd see him, he'd always say: "Hey, how's my big brother's best friend?"

I had found the keys to the kingdom, right in my own pocket.

First acting role in *the Black Klansman (I Crossed the Color Line)*.

CHAPTER 7

"HIRE HIM, HENRY!"

Not to belabor the point, but I had climbed right into the penthouse of Hollywood, me, a guy with no major acting bona fides who had an office on the lot, studio privileges, and a seven-year contract with the biggest studio in the business. I wasn't making big money; three hundred bucks a week didn't get you far in L.A., even then. If I recall, the contract quickly ran up to a couple of grand a week. But even before that, if I had wanted to travel to, say, China, on a lark, I could have used my executive code number and been on the next flight to Hong Kong or some other foreign place. I didn't try it, but I did give it serious thought a couple of times.

Meanwhile, the roles just kept on coming. One more that came along in 1968 was *If He Hollers, Let Him Go!* a convoluted murder mystery that put black actors in roles as whores and deceitful criminals. This was an independent film—my contract gave me the freedom to do movies for other studios, another thing I can rightly brag about, since it was so rare during the studio system era. This allowed me to pad my résumé quite frequently.

These moonlighting roles generally were in movies with black, culturally important themes. This was in the aftermath of the murder of Martin Luther King, Jr., and, in a sign of the times, the blockbuster *In the Heat of the Night* hit theaters. Sidney Poitier, playing a cop partnered with Rod Steiger's southern redneck sheriff, marked perhaps the first-time a black character wasn't compromised by playing second fiddle to a white star. With racial sensibilities heightened, Hollywood suddenly wanted blacks to be men, not shadows of other men, their displays of anger righteous, not threatening to an entire race. So, when *If He Hollers* was made, it seemed like it could be a landmark film, given that black actors—good black actors, like Raymond St. Jacques and Barbara McNair—were cast in it.

My part was again small, a few lines as the defense attorney for a black man framed for murder. It was written and directed by a guy named Charles Martin, whose previous credits included a light Esther Williams comedy in 1948, which included stereotypical black "natives" on a Pacific Island looking to put white people in a pot of stew. That probably should have been a tip-off that he was not exactly an ideal bearer of black culture, but I went ahead hoping for the best. Sadly, the best never came. Rather, no matter how well intentioned, it was an echo of *I Crossed the Color Line*, with blacks depicted as loose women and savages. It failed, on merit, and I was grateful not to be associated with, or listed in the credits of, what Roger Ebert called "ugly," "trash," and "insulting garbage" that "does not in any sense treat [the black] actors with dignity or even decency," citing its "two cheaply exploited angles: nudity and racism." The only benefit of being in another *I Crossed the Color Line* debacle was that it introduced me to Raymond St. Jacques and Barbara McNair, two eminently qualified members of the guild.

By contrast, another film that year showed how themes relevant to blacks and society should be done. *Uptight* was directed by Jules Dassin for Paramount. Jules, a survivor of the pernicious Hollywood red-scare blacklists of the '50s, which forced him to make movies in Europe until the mid-sixties, had a strength for gritty noir crime films, like *The Naked City*, and heist films, like *Rififi*. Being in one of his rare American productions was a privilege, and I leaped at his reworking of John Ford's 1935 film *The Informer* about the Irish Revolution, the plot centering on an ill-fated revolutionary informing on the black militant sect he had founded. They filmed on location in Cleveland, and there were some unbelievable black actors cast: Raymond St. Jacques, Ruby Dee, Roscoe Lee Browne—and guess who else? None other than Max Julien, two years after his film debut in *I Crossed the Color Line*. I played a militant named Mello—getting on-screen credit—and Jules didn't hedge on the dialogue; it was raw, angry. In many ways, it set the course for the blaxploitation era, although with realism, not escapism or caricatures. There was no self-parody. I had intense scenes, such as holding back an anguished Ketty Lester, a rather good singer and actress, from attacking a character named Tank, played by Julian Mayfield, who also co-wrote the movie.

That was my first credited role in a major movie, and I took a lot from it. The movie wasn't a big hit, but viewers and critics believed that these were real black people on the screen, and some of the critics mentioned an observation they found disturbing: Audiences both black and white broke into cheering when a black character killed a white one. This was turning on its head the former custom of white audiences cheering the killing of black characters, invariably the "bad guys." Here, seeming bad guys were good guys, a barometer of how society was changing, as whites were beginning to see the world through the eyes of black people.

Meanwhile, I continued to take an assortment of small television parts for Universal, CBS, and Paramount Studios. I barely had time to rest between scenes. I would run into Don McElwaine, Tom Jennings, or Sid Sheinberg, and if there was a TV pilot being shot, they would send me over there. That happened with a whole string of shows—*The Good Guys* with Bob "Gilligan" Denver and Herb Edelman, *Mannix* with Mike Connors, *Hawaii Five-O* with Jack Lord, *The Outsider* with Darren McGavin, *The Wild Wild West* with Robert Conrad, and *The Protectors*, starring Leslie Nielsen and Hari Rhodes as crime-fighters, with Hari as one of the earliest black co-stars of a TV show. I played a character named Noah on *The Protectors*—although society at the time was still having a little trouble identifying black actors.

The Herald-Examiner ran a promo for the show when the pilot episode, "Deadlock," ran, with a photo captioned: "James McEachin, featured on 'Deadlock,' Channel 4 at 9 p.m." Except the photo was of the white comedian Frank Gorshin. I still have that clipping.

The funny thing was, TV was so much more important than the movies then, and many of the people who were in the TV elite seemed to believe they owned Hollywood. Jack Lord, star of *Hawaii Five-O*, for example: He ran that show like he was an Army officer, and apparently, I had been court-martialed again. I was given the role of a police chaplain, Captain John Anderson, and off to Honolulu I went.

The director, a short guy named Seymour Robbie, who I thought was highly creative, thought it might be a good idea to give the chaplain some character, make him tougher.

"Good," I half-joked, "'Cause I ain't so hot at playing chaplains. Throws my rhythm off."

"Do you smoke? he asked.

"Like a train."

"Good. Light 'em up."

I did. We started rehearsing the scene, and Jack drove up. He spotted me, the chaplain, smoking a cigarette. Jack looked like he was about to explode.

"You're a chaplain, a preacher!" he bellowed. "You are not going to smoke on my show. In fact, you are not going to be on my show! Just wait'll CBS hears about this!"

Knowing that wasn't dialogue from the script, I started looking for the director, hoping for the man of inventiveness and courage to speak up. But Seymour had quickly hidden himself behind a big 10K lamp, out of Jack's range of fire. And, instead of just saying, "Okay, just put out the cigarette, let's get back to the scene," he kowtowed to Jack. That night, back in my hotel room, I got a call telling me to be on the 8:00 a.m. flight out of Hawaii the next morning. I didn't even care. That was a rotten thing to do, to any actor, of any color. But if he was going to be that irrational, that was his problem; I wouldn't engage. Besides, I had so many logs on the fire that there would be ten jobs waiting for me. Maybe he wanted me to grovel. I do not grovel. Never have, never will.

This won't surprise you, but that was not the last time I was fired.

Jack Lord was just one of a plethora of people in Hollywood who believed that the world revolved around them and their shows. If he was any different, perhaps that show wouldn't have run for twelve years and 281 episodes, winning two Emmys during its tenure. I never judged anyone by their success or failure. I made friends with just about everyone in Hollywood, yet I never spoke with Jack Lord again. Good riddance, to Jack and to Seymour Robbie, who I figured was still in hiding when I landed back in L.A.

The TV carousel kept on turning, so fast that I don't remember all the roles with which I am credited. There was one called *The Outsider* starring Darren McGavin. Produced by *The Fugitive* creator Roy Huggins, it was a private-eye caper, the twist being that he had been pardoned for a crime. The role had originally been offered to Jack Lord, who turned it down to do *Hawaii Five-O*. I am said to have played someone named John Arnold, but I have no earthly memory of being on the show at all—though I'm sure I knocked it out of the park.

I do remember being on *The Wild Wild West* as a secret agent because Bobby Conrad was unforgettable to be around. What times we used to have! Bobby had the most fun with a role of anyone I've ever seen. For him, work had to be fun, or he'd cut out, and that quality really showed through on the screen. He didn't have to kill himself memorizing scripts; like they say Jackie Gleason used to do, he'd give it a once-over and he knew the lines. Moreover, he could turn a spoof into a dramatic story. Think about that famous battery commercial he did, when he looked into the camera and said, "Go ahead, knock this battery off my shoulder. Dare ya." It was funny, but frightening, because he was a tough guy, a brawler; he'd fight you in a second if he got pissed off. But he was also a guy who would take whoever was around him, even guys he belted around, to the closest bar and buy everybody rounds. He'd meet his buddy, Doug McClure, who was doing a lot of TV work—and would later do a pilot with me—and they were a wrecking crew. They were both young, virile, good-looking guys with money. You can assume where that lead.

Movies would interrupt the TV work, which kept my batteries fresher. The next one, late in '69, was *True Grit*, a major vehicle for John Wayne, who was sixty-two at the time and wanted to prove he was still as strong and commanding as ever. The studio was Paramount, the producer Hal Wallis, the director Henry Hathaway, who had worked with Duke on several previous movies. They were all mega-heavyweights, but they didn't intimidate me. When I got to the studio, I walked across the stage and said, "Mr. Hathaway, I'm here for the role of the hanging judge's bailiff.

And he said, "Well, can you act?"

What was I supposed to say? So, I steeled myself and said, "Yeah, better than anyone else here can." And before he could say anything, I heard a voice bark from in the dark behind the cameras.

"Hire him, Henry!"

The bark, I recognized immediately, was that of John Wayne.

From that moment on, Duke and I became friends. He was in every way larger than life. Tall, assured, that crooked smirk letting you know he was just plain folks. Even as he aged and began wearing toupees, he exuded masculinity. And he took a liking to me. During the shooting of *True Grit*, he told me flat out, "You're gonna do my next picture." I laughed at that.

I didn't get on-screen credit for *True Grit*, which was entirely the doing of the moon-faced Henry Hathaway, a hugely respected director within the Western genre but also, to be blunt, a racist. Totally. The movie was about U.S. Marshal Rooster Cogburn, the grizzled, eye-patched Texas Ranger who tracks down the killer of a young girl's father by riding with her into Indian country. The cast was almost all white, led by Duke, Kim Darby, Robert Duvall, Dennis Hopper, Jeff Corey, and the singer Glen Campbell, who was cast after Elvis Presley turned down the part. Henry seemingly didn't want to dilute the credits by including me, although he made room for Ken Renard, a native of Trinidad, who played an Indian, as light-skinned black actors sometimes did.

Henry made no secret of despising me, more so because I was" uppity" to him, disobeying his directions about how to play the part of a court bailiff. I had one line— "Rooster J. Cogburn will take the stand." He wanted me to play it subserviently, say the lines lazy and whiny. I refused over and over. I said, "No, I'm not gonna do that. I don't do Butterfly McQueen." I could tell that Duke was enjoying my resistance, and this experience contradicted the latter-day accusations that Duke was a racist. Attitudes towards racial equality were changing and Duke was admittedly out of step with the times. In a 1971 *Playboy* interview he said that "we can't all of a sudden get down on our knees and turn everything over to the leadership of the blacks" and "I believe in white supremacy until the blacks are educated to a point of responsibility."

I certainly can't condone those ignorant statements, but I can vouch for Duke, the man I knew.

He was complicated, as most of us are, and a product of another era, but also a victim of them. I do not believe he was a racist, and he gave a lot of money to good causes. But he had hardened views, and a leopard doesn't change its spots. I found him to be a funny guy, but never did I hear him tell a racist joke, something that was oh-so-common in Hollywood, even among liberals. Duke was a hardboiled guy with a soft side who would spend hours spinning yarns about Hollywood. He would get away, live out in the hinter- lands. He married three times to Mexican or South American women. He was reckless, whether it was with women, drinking, whatever. What I— me— James McEachin—can say about John Wayne is that he never uttered a racist word to or around me and, in fact, he sided with me against Henry.

Duke was the last giant. He was the only reason why *True Grit* made $31 million. He won his only Oscar and would make a sequel, *Rooster Cogburn*, in 1975. In terms of my part, I was grateful that I hadn't been a ludicrous cliché. It was another small step forward, for me and all black actors. Despite not receiving a credit on-screen. A final irony, or perhaps not, is that Henry's final film was a stunningly bad blaxploitation movie about ruthless ghetto gangs causing needless mayhem, released under the title *Hangup,* and later retitled *Super Dude.*

This was how a man like Henry saw black people, but Duke didn't. I'm not saying he was a saint, but he didn't like hypocrisy, and neither did I. What he felt he needed to say, he said, even if everyone else disagreed with him. In some ways, he was the caricature people made him out to be. The times were changing too fast for men like him; the real world was tougher for him to live in than the world that he could control in a movie script. But it was in his role as a movie star par excellence that I knew him, and in which he wanted me to be with him.

A year later, Duke kept his word about me being in his next movie and gave me a role in *The Undefeated*, another Old West story situated just after the Civil War. Duke plays an ex-Union officer who teams up with Rock Hudson as an ex-Confederate officer to fight off Mexican revolutionaries. I played an opportunistic carpetbagger named Jimmy Collins—I laugh thinking of the name because when I was sent the script for the movie, it wasn't addressed to me but to "Jimmy Collins." I had to call the Twentieth Century Fox production office and ask if it was sent to the wrong guy. They said Duke wanted me to get used to being Jimmy Collins. The production company sent me a plane ticket to Baton Rouge, Louisiana, where they were already in the process of shooting on an old slave plantation. When the people down there heard that John Wayne was coming to do a movie, they were partying in the streets like it was a hootenanny. One day, I was standing with Duke in the yard of the main house, and people were coming over asking for his autograph, damn near trampling me to get near him. Duke very politely told them, "Can't you see I'm talking to this gentleman?" Duke was a class act.

In one scene of the film, Rock's character, Col. Langdon, says to Henry Beckman's character, Thad Benedict, "This house is not for sale, not now, not next year, not ever. You're trash!" Benedict looks over to Jimmy and says, "Hear what the man said, Jimmy?" Jimmy Collins then rattles off the practical realities of the Langdons staying on the property, without, thanks to the recent Emancipation Proclamation, the bevy of slaves who previously ran the plantation. Jimmy asks, "Who's gonna pick your cotton, and who's gonna plow up all that bottomland out there, and who's gonna chop the wood when it gets cold?" For just a moment, Jimmy forces the ex-Confederate soldier to reassess his assumptions about black men being ignorant. That was a kick. Actually, though, the plot was secondary to the two old war-horses who knew how to eat the scenery, which the director Andy McLaglen was perfectly content to let them do.

Between filming one day, when we were on set at the plantation, Duke said to me, "Jim, listen. Go down to the basement. That's where they kept the slaves back then. You have to see it. You really need to see it, Keach, you really do." I could tell by the look on his face that he had been touched by what he saw down below. Earlier, long before filming started, Duke must have taken a look-see while the company was scouting and prepping, like production does when on location. I bet he was alone, taking a sightseeing tour of the grounds. He was a garrulous man, a generous man, but he didn't care too much for company. You could feel it. That said, he would defend his friends to the hilt—which was why it was no surprise when, upon the owner of the house returning, cussing, and demanding to know why I was in the house, Duke cut him off at the pass: "Don't go there. You're about to insult one of the finest actors in our business. Say another word and we'll tear this whole goddamn thing down!"

Duke was right, too, about my seeing the place. I did need to see it. When I made my way down those cellar stairs, in a way it became the beginning of a life-altering experience. As I walked around the clay floor of this musty old windowless room, I could only gaze silently at chains and hooks dangling from the walls, which no one had thought to clear away in over a hundred years, and which seemed to groan with the pain of guilt and wince with the stench of death. I could almost feel the presence of slaves who had lived, been tortured, and died in that room. If only those walls could talk, I thought. How many human beings with skin the color of my own had been chained together, barely able to move or breathe, kept hungry, abused in every way?

The impact of standing where they had once stood scarred my consciousness; those souls who had their heritage and families taken from them stayed with me for years and came to life when I wrote *Tell Me A Tale*. I would read dozens of books about slavery in my research, yet nothing written on a page could make me feel the terror they must have felt, the optimism they sang of in their spirituals, and the vengeance they sought—the final impulse of *Tell Me A Tale*. I was imbued with emotion as I stood in that room, and I know that John Wayne, the man some would call a racist, had felt something similar when he stood in that cellar. That is why I say that he was a complicated man, more complicated than anyone knew. A final word about this good man. He had a bout with cancer. As a matter of fact, we both did. For me, two of them. I believe those travails made each of us more of a man: real men, not dramatis personae on a silver screen.

Rock Hudson was another quintessential good guy. In fact, he, too, was moved by the fact that people there were descended from former slaves. We hired some of the locals as extras and gave them tax forms and day-player contracts that they didn't know how to read and weren't able to sign their names to; it was as if time had stood still. Rock would have conversations with them. One was an elderly man who could barely walk, and Rock dug in his pocket and extracted a gold watch worth thousands of dollars and unceremoniously gave it to the old man.

Rock had complexities that he concealed by playing breezy, insouciant romantic leads with Doris Day and other women. Few outside of the Hollywood coterie knew he was gay at the time. Certainly, I didn't, nor would I have cared, but I can imagine how it ate him up inside. Rock told me one time about an old friend of his who he asked to house-sit for him when Rock went to Europe to do a movie. The guy brought his family out and stayed at Rock's house in Beverly Hills, but when Rock got home, no one was there. The friend had cleared out with no word as to why. Rock believed it was because the friend got jealous of Rock being able to live in splendor, as if Rock was rubbing it in. That irked Rock because he never lorded his wealth and status over anyone, least of all his friends. He was one of the humblest people I ever knew.

It may be why people took great advantage of him, exerting some form of influence over him as a price for keeping his secret. People he trusted exploited him, such as notorious, in-the-closet casting directors who made liberal use of the casting couch. I thought there was a sadness to him, and that he may have liked those romantic leads as an escape to live someone else's life. Keep in mind the stakes that were involved, how many millions of dollars the studios might have lost if his secret got out. Imagine the pressure the man lived under to keep his sexual preference quiet. Case in point: I was with Robert Wagner one night, and we went into the Cock and Bull, a bar in L.A. where stars liked to congregate. In a dark corner, Bobby saw Rock, an old friend of his, sitting alone, wearing a fake beard, alone with his thoughts, drowning his sorrows.

When he died of AIDS years later, the press focused on only on his being gay, it was a condemnation; I thought it was the most unfair thing ever done to any man, because he never would have done harm to any other person and didn't deserve to be treated as he was. I still feel anger about that.

The Undefeated was a disappointment for the studio. It cost $10 million to make and barely broke even at the box office. It was a sign that the old guard was dying, though Duke would keep trying to retain his title and wanted me to be a part of his continuing string of movies. For now, I went on notching roles, very much aware that I had helped make larger strides for black actors. That responsibility weighed heavily on my mind. I had become disenchanted with the scripts that white producers and directors, in their ignorance and conditioned racism, believed were positive markers for blacks.

Two made-for-TV movies that had not been offered to me were *Carter's Army* and *My Sweet Charlie*, broadcast a week apart early in 1970 on ABC and NBC, respectively. The subject matter of each was compelling. The former, a war drama set in Germany, depicted a redneck officer in charge of an all-black unit (something I knew a bit about), and its cast included a veritable who's-who of black talent: Robert Hooks, Moses Gunn, Billy Dee Williams, Glynn Turman, and a young Richard Pryor. Of course, they all go into battle and become the model of brotherhood—a fable I had actually experienced in Korea, but not with the ease and simplicity of these characters. *My Sweet Charlie*, which had had a brief Broadway run, tells of a black activist attorney, played by Al Freeman, Jr., who escapes after being falsely accused of a murder and goes on the run with a white pregnant girl, played by Patty Duke.

That I was ignored for the juicy black roles in these vehicles may have been because the studio knew I would be rankled by the scripts. When I saw the movies, I knew I would have turned them down. To the crowned heads at the studio, these entries were something to revel in; *Charlie*, which had enormous potential, was a runaway ratings winner and received numerous Emmy nominations, with Patty winning for best actress and Al, a fine actor, making black history being nominated for best actor. It won the NAACP's Image Award. A black publicist, Walter Burrell, who had gotten his job through pressure on Universal by the Urban League to hire more blacks, didn't agree with the praise the movie was receiving. He had taken the job in the hope of heralding a new era of reality-based programming, and *Charlie* was antithetical to that. After the release of *Charlie*, Walter strayed from the ranch and wrote a review in Ebony savaging the films as trite and mindless, stripping the black characters of a true black identity, and turning them pseudo-white. I agreed with him, but his review was not at all appreciated by the Universal brass. Word was that he would be fired, basically for being too black. I found that example of rank hypocrisy truer to life than those movies were. Sadly, although I told Walter I had his back, I could not keep him from losing his job, though he did fine as a Hollywood columnist until his death in 1990. More tragically, a half-century later, TV is still filled with examples of what white executives think black people are like and how they act, often as blithering idiots. I believe there has been only one black executive in all of entertainment through the years who could really get things done: Stanley Robertson. Stanley was a vice president of NBC back then, and he wasn't just window dressing: he had juice. He could seal a deal. After leaving NBC, Stanley later held high offices at Universal and Columbia Pictures. Though nearly blind, he had the vision to produce some important, black-oriented shows and movies, a genre that had become all but invisible in a world of screeching, leering, cursing, bug-eyed black vaudevillians that began with Jimmie Walker's "J. J." character on *Good Times*. Stanley was responsible for creating the first television drama featuring a black family, *Harris and Company*. He also later oversaw the minority hiring program at Columbia Pictures. But Stanley had his problems, too, some profoundly serious problems, though he managed to weather the storms with fortitude and continued as one of the top black executives in the business.

If I gained a reputation as a shoot-from-the-lip black man as a result of sticking my nose where it wasn't supposed to be, it did nothing to stem my own upward ascent, to the point where I was virtually the "go-to" guy for TV parts calling for a fortyish, wizened old black who could best comically inept white men—the new stereotype of Caucasians created by the small minds of the industry. As an actor, I was in no position to change anything in a script; all I could do was make a role as real and convincing as possible with how I performed the lines. I could never have been a white man's black man.

Some directors came to know that I wasn't all that threatening and that the fast lane was opening for more blacks. There was a time when I was doing so many roles that one day (I think it was for Viacom), I literally did a scene for one show in the morning, then one for another in the afternoon, and still another in the evening. To some, I was considered a good luck charm because usually, when I did a pilot, the show would sell.

One of those was *Then Came Bronson*, an archetypal antihero saga with a James Dean-type, Michael Parks, as a guy who gives up a comfortable lifestyle to find adventure riding his motorcycle on the open road, a takeoff of the movie *Easy Rider*. I happened to be one of the characters he encountered, Spud the Pool Shark. Hey, it was work, it was real, and I got the chance to chew up some scenery. The part was small, but when I added my own touches, based on the pool sharks I grew up with in Hackensack, the directors were more than quick to make the role larger. Unfortunately, Bronson only lasted a season; fortunately, I lasted a little longer, because the real meat of this accidental career was just around the corner of my own adventurous route, within a dizzying span of only three years that took me squarely to the intersections of the good, the bad, and the ugly.

Marian McCargo, Henry Beckman, and James on the set of The Undefeated

Played Mello in Up Tight, first credited role

CHAPTER 8

MISTY WATERCOLOR MEMORIES

TV was the lifeblood of most everything Universal did. Movies were catching up, but even the movie projects that came over the transom were seen by Lew Wasserman and Sid Sheinberg through the lens of a TV camera. The pilot episode for many shows were "made-for-TV movies," as the genre was called. One of those in 1968 was *It Takes a Thief*, which had the cool veneer of international playboy trappings, which were required in the era inspired by the James Bond craze. Massive ratings hits, like *I Spy* and *The Man from U.N.C.L.E.*, made it conceivable that even a cat burglar could be recruited by the government to steal secrets of enemy governments, a role that became Robert Wagner's, as Alexander Mundy, for three seasons. I was in an early episode, "The Galloping Skin Game," as Earl Danton, a semi-crazed bodyguard for Mundy's pal Nick Grobbo, nicely played by Ricardo Montalban. For the role I used a sinister Jamaican accent and struck a pose like a praying mantis, clasping my hands as if in prayer as I cradled a knife with a long blade. I would draw out my words, delivering lines such as, "I . . . will . . . kill . . you." I created all these touches and was rewarded with three more episodes of *Thief*. Whatever was needed, I did it. I still wasn' making much, but it was always an education to be able to study great actors. Late in the show's run, they brought in Fred Astaire as Mundy's father. I had known Fred from his music publishing company, but now I could watch him as he effortlessly read lines; they even made him the star of several episodes, making Bobby a supporting actor in those.

The most valuable inroad I made on these TV excursions—only detouring once for a movie, an uncredited bit part thanks to actor/director and pal, Gene Kelly, in the screen version of *Hello, Dolly*—was working with the inimitable Jack Webb, for the institution that was *Dragnet*. In the 1950s, *Dragnet* set the gold standard for TV detective shows. While Sergeant Joe Friday's world of clipped dialogue, wooden characters, and uncomplicated stories ("Taken from the files of the LAPD," as the narrator intoned) seemed completely anachronistic in the late 1960s and early '70s, Jack somehow knew how to make *Dragnet* work. Many dismissed him as a far right-wing moralist with no tolerance for cultural change, and he was that, but Jack knew that even the most rebellious young people were suckers for a good moral drama. The oversimplified, "Just the facts, ma'am" plots, which he had to approve every word of, always delivered—sometimes with comical effect, such as when Sgt. Friday runs into "hippies," mocking their lingo even though it had become commonplace. The fact was, Jack Webb himself existed in a suspended reality, and he loved it. Taken out of it, he would have been lost.

Anyone acting on *Dragnet* had to adhere to his rules, which I learned when I did my first episode, "Homicide: The Student," in September 1969. I played Jake Mahler; the gym coach of a student suspected of being a sniper. We went through the dialogue over and over. Jack would direct the episodes, and only he could get the actors to perform the dialogue in that familiar staccato monotone that you had to learn if you did the show. That was how Jack Webb spoke even in real life—machine-gun style, trading off quick, clipped sentences with another actor in a sort of duet, repeating the last few words of the last speaker as a question. It was almost comical, and was often parodied by comedians, but man, did it work well in a police drama. When I finished my scene, he looked at me with that hard stare of his and said in his stiff manner of speech, "It was crap." But he said it with a sly twinkle in the eye. I am guessing he knew I was still new at acting and that he had to do something to improve my performance. He kept it well hidden, but Jack had a real understanding of acting, something he was very much underrated for.

A tough director to work for, he walked ramrod straight, his arms not moving, stuck to his sides; he reminded one of a toy soldier. A lot of people called him stiff or cardboard, and ridiculed *Dragnet*'s lack of frills or action, but Jack laughed all the way to the bank with the money he saved on set decorators. My God, walking onto that set was like walking into a prison. Everyone, the cast, crew, all of them were scared to death of Jack Webb. NBC never sent a guy to observe the filming of *Dragnet*, as all the networks did, because no one wanted to risk getting in his way. Jack wanted quiet, and the set was like a morgue.

There was almost no action in *Dragnet*; the dialogue was the nucleus, and it had to be exactly right, framed by extreme close-ups and feverish cutting from one character to another. The actors had to mesh like singers in a duet, all voices becoming one, handing off the lead to each other. If you tried improvising, he would stop you in your tracks. If my line was, "Listen, you're under arrest," and I instead said, "Well, listen, you're under arrest," Jack would stop me: "Don't put a 'well' in there! Keep it straight. Just the line." Follow the rules and you'd get parts, no matter if the viewers recognized you from an earlier role. Only a month after I played Jake Mahler, I was playing Dr. Collins, then after that Officer Tim Miles. It didn't matter to Jack. You weren't really there as a character—only Sgt. Friday and his partner Officer Gannon, played to perfection by Harry Morgan, were set in stone; everyone else was a side man in a jazz band.

Jack was in character even off stage, although he would allow himself a laugh here and there. After we finished shooting an episode, he would take three or four of the cast or crew to a bar for a cocktail. He would meet up with his ex-wife, Julie London and her husband, Bobby Troup, both of whom were now actors, but who I first knew when Julie was a chanteuse in the '50s singing in nightclubs and Bobby was writing pop songs. They were his closest friends, closer than Jack was to his girlfriend at the time, who he would allow to see him only one day a week. We'd have a few drinks, unwind, and Jack would let his hair down—which is to say, not much, given his trademark buzzcut.

He was direct, insanely focused, and the rewards for his focus were many, one being that *Dragnet* was commemorated on a postage stamp. Perhaps because he wrote, produced, directed, and starred in any number of episodes, he made more money than any other producer on Universal's lot, plus he had interest in other shows. He was one of the smartest men in the business. Jack Webb didn't work for Mark VII productions: He owned it. One day, to prove the efficacy of his style of shooting and the ability to cut costs at the same time, he shot an entire episode of *Dragnet* in one day, a feat virtually unheard of when dealing with the Big Three networks. Jack was also known for paying a generous wage, up to a couple thousand dollars per episode. That's why actors who hated Jack's politics loved Jack the producer.

Jack was always the embodiment of Sgt. Joe Friday, and if he befriended you, you were a friend for life. He invited me out to his house, which was—much like Jack—down to earth. In his den he kept a prodigious record collection and played them on state-of-the art stereo equipment. I would have expected him to be a fan of Lawrence Welk, Bing Crosby, the Andrews Sisters. Instead, I was shocked to see a collection of just about every jazz record ever made. Jack was the biggest devotee of jazz I ever knew. He could lecture on the relative merits and subtle differences of Charlie Parker, Miles Davis, Louis Armstrong, Billie Holiday: all the greats. I'm sure his ear for jazz licks played into the rhythmic dialogue of *Dragnet*. Jack told me that all his life he wanted to be a jazz disc jockey, and that the best role he ever had was to play a jazz cornetist and bandleader in *Pete Kelly's Blues*, first on the radio in his pre-*Dragnet* days, then in the 1955 movie that he also directed and produced and that co-starred Peggy Lee. Jack put together all the music for the movie, which was a big hit, making $5 million for Mark VII.

Being in with Jack Webb brought real benefits, not only roles in *Dragnet*. For a time, if I wasn't doing *Dragnet*, I was doing *Adam-12*, the cop show Jack created for Universal in 1968, which ran for seven seasons. It was meant to attract a young audience, with two younger, better-looking Joe Fridays, played by Martin Milner and Kent McCord, with some at-home subplots, buddy humor, and car chases to broaden the ritual of catching bad guys in L.A. There were also ample parts for black actors—not always with the best of intentions, which soon became evident, with me right there as a witness.

I did six episodes of *Adam-12*, two as cops, two as jive-talkin' boxing gym owner Freddy Rivers, and one as the watch commander Lieutenant Moore, an integral part in the early life of the series that had been played by a white actor. However, my most memorable role was that of a black militant gang member named Dewey Randolph in "Log

76: The Militants." Having played roles as black militants before, I was sensitive to the way white screenwriters and directors had often portrayed black men who gave voice to their grievances. Most scripts then made blacks too subservient, yet when playing militants, they were automatically "bad guys" with no redeeming values. There seemed very little daylight between what was militant and justifiable, and when a white writer such as Art Names tried to take the black side, it was badly botched.

Unfortunately, I was in no position to turn down scripts, much less make a fuss about characters I had a problem with—something I was able to do a bit later, when I castigated a certain *Roots*-like TV series before it even aired. In the early '70s, however, I wasn't there yet, even if I could see that the *Adam-12* script was problematic—depicting militants as calculating killers trying to frame a cop for a murder of their own doing. Still, I respected Jack Webb to no end and trusted that his only motivation was to portray a realistic story, and I did the episode. I didn't judge him, just as I didn't judge John Wayne for his racially charged remarks. I only knew these giants were fair with me, and I do believe if I wanted to direct a show, Jack would have provided the avenue.

In a sense, I lived with blinders on, like a horse racing down the track, seeing only the finish line. I would see all those giant photographs of stars on the wall of the Universal commissary and want my mug to be up there—which it would be.

I did another TV movie called *The Brotherhood of the Bell* starring Glenn Ford and Dean Jagger, two old pros who rarely did TV. It was the kind of psychological thriller made by Orson Welles in the '40s, and which would thrill today's conspiracy theory-spewing crowd. A professor, played by Glenn, whose past membership in a secret society of rich oligarchs that controls the government, tries to expose it as it tries to destroy him; his is a lonely fight, as everyone around him thinks he's paranoid. I played—guess what? —a cop, a detective to be exact.

Next up, in quick succession, were roles on *The Name of the Game*, the umbrella title for three ninety-minute mystery movies produced by Universal for NBC, rotating weekly around the stars Gene

Barry, Robert Stack, and Tony Franciosa, whose playboy socialite characters worked in different capacities for a publishing empire. Fittingly, the show had the largest budget of any TV series, and the music was scored by the great jazzman, Dave Grusin. Not only was it cool and a ratings winner, it was also where Steven Spielberg, at just twenty-four, broke in as a director. On the 1971 episode "L.A. 2017," which was more apocalyptic science fiction than jet-setting intrigue, Steven used clever camera angles, making clear what his strength was. Another beneficiary of the series was not-yet-thirty Steven Bochco, a somewhat Spielberg lookalike who had a hand in writing some episodes, the springboard to his reign as Universal's top screenwriter on such powerhouse shows as *Columbo* and *Ironside* before going to MTM Productions and Fox and developing the biggest TV hits of the '80s including *Hill Street Blues*, *L.A. Law*, and *NYPD Blue*.

Considering that it only ran for three years, *Name of the Game* was a remarkable treasure trove of budding movers and shakers. As for me, I did four episodes as typical streetwise types. These roles raised my profile—and bank account—quite nicely, but the biggest benefit was that I met and got to know writer and producer Dean Hargrove, a wonderful man, on his way to bigger and better things. Tall and gentlemanly—the latter a real rarity in the business—he was tapped by Universal to write a new pilot about the rumpled, raincoat-wearing, seemingly-confused homicide detective, Columbo, three years after the original pilot—developed by Dick Levinson and Bill Link—failed to fly. That, too, became a pot of gold (with Spielberg also directing an early episode) and Dean parlayed it into more opportunities, producing *Columbo* and then other gems, like *Matlock*, *Jake and the Fatman*, and *Diagnosis: Murder*. He always kept me in mind for parts on these historic markers, which would help determine my future, and I am happy to say that Dean and I are still close friends—also a rarity in this business.

Being within the ranks of these young up-and-comers, and a couple of old ones, provided even more opportunity. Look closely and you'll see me in most of the top shows for the next two decades. The TV spigot brought *The Senator* (yet another chance to work with Hal Holbrook), *The F.B.I.* (which, like *Dragnet*, was based on real crime cases, with the same clipped acting style, even if Efrem Zimbalist, Jr., couldn't quite emulate Jack's rhythmic meter), *The Sixth Sense* (in which a college professor solves mysteries using extra-sensory perception, each episode introduced by *The Twilight Zone*'s Rod Serling), and *Men at Law*, about storefront lawyers, starring Robert Foxworth. In most of these roles, I was even-tempered, in control, never trying to steal a scene from the stars, which I'm sure they appreciated. Only when I believed a black man in real life would blow a fuse did I allow my character to lose his cool. The directors didn't mind. If I wanted to smoke a cigarette and blow smoke in someone's face, I could do it.

Conversely, whenever Jack Webb had another part for me, I went into restrained *Dragnet* mode, such as when Jack created another show— (and rarely did a year go by when he didn't)—for Universal, starring David Janssen, who needed a series after *The Fugitive* ended his epochal role as the man on the run. In his new role on *O'Hara, U.S. Treasury*, he played a treasury agent fighting white-collar crime, like tax fraud. Jack tried jazzing it up by hiring Dave Brubeck for the music score, but it was not the most exciting premise. David never seemed to be that interested in the series, and it lasted only one season, proving that not even Jack and David could overcome a show about a treasury agent. But David was a sweetheart of a guy. He even gave his mother a bit part in the show. The show did get a Golden Globe nomination, mainly on David's aura, and he could always reach out and reel in another part.

Meanwhile, the movie parts—made-for-TV and theatrical—continued to come to me. One of the former, *D.A.: Conspiracy to Kill*, was a Universal pilot starring Robert Conrad as a perceptive D.A. piecing together murder cases, and Bobby wanted me as a character named Eddie Jewell. He had high hopes for it, but even his popularity couldn't rouse enough of an audience, a rare defeat for him, though he would be back in the game before too long. Another TV movie, *The Neon Ceiling*, starring Gig Young and Lee Grant, had me as a highway patrolman, a blink-and-you'd-miss-me part. I had begun to think these steady but unheralded parts would never lead to anything truly memorable. And then, as if by cue, the trajectory of my career changed, thanks to Clint Eastwood.

The story of *Play Misty for Me* begins with a call from Bob LaSanka, a Universal casting director who was casting for a new Clint

Eastwood film to be produced by Bob Daley. It would mark Clint's directorial debut. It would be set at a radio station, with the title taken from Erroll Garner's 1954 instrumental jazz hit "Misty," and a few years later made into a pop hit by Johnny Mathis, who added the lyrics about being as helpless as a kitten up a tree. The song had been covered dozens of times, and disc jockeys were inundated with requests from listeners to "play 'Misty' for me."

That was the premise of the script Clint's Malpaso production company optioned from a former model and dancer, Jo Heims, and had expanded by screenwriter Dean Riesner into a full-blown psychological thriller. We all know the story, about a psycho stalker played by Jessica Walter, who would call Clint, a DJ at a local jazz radio station, and make the same request, planning to bed and then kill him with a long shiny knife. Clint set the film in Carmel, California, where he lived in real life (and would later serve as mayor) and shot it on location there. He gave Don Siegel a part as a bartender so he could have Don available for directorial advice. The rest of the casting was in the hands of Bob LaSanka, and Bob had me in mind.

"I got a role for you," he told me one day at Universal. "Go over and see Bob Daley at Malpaso."

Although I didn't get to know Clint when we made *Coogan's Bluff*, apparently, he knew me as a reliable actor who had worked in the music business, two qualifications that led Clint to consider me for an important role in his new movie. I high tailed it over there to see Daley and, while I was waiting, who else but Clint came in. He asked who I was, but I could tell he already knew me by the grin he was fighting. "You dirty dog," I said. "I didn't know who you were before *Coogan's Bluff*, and you didn't know me. Now you gonna make me tell you who I am?"

He let the grin spread and said, "I can't fool you, Mr. McEachin," and shook my hand. Then we sat down, and he had a question for me. He said he had a song he wanted to use in the movie, "The First Time Ever I Saw Your Face," the superb, sensuous ballad by Roberta Flack. He wanted to know what I thought of it. I said I loved the song.

"Is that your professional opinion?" he asked.

"Well," I said, "I just happen to have been in the music business. I was Jimmy Mack, and I sure as hell know what I'm talkin' about."

This was before many had heard the Flack version, which was on her 1969 debut album. Clint, who, like Jack Webb, knew and loved jazz, heard it while listening to a jazz radio station. For me to know the song influenced Clint, originally, he had wanted to use another song, a Motown song. But Motown was going to charge him a lot and Clint was monitoring every penny. To get Lew Wasserman to okay the project initially, he had to agree to direct without any additional pay, but it was worth it to him. "First Time" came cheaper than the Motown song, costing Clint only $2,000, but he had to know it would strike the right mood. My opinion helped him decide. The song was played during a steamy amour scene with his character's girlfriend, well played by Donna Mills. Including the tune in the movie propelled it to number one on the charts for six weeks, and it won the Grammy in 1972 for best song. So, maybe I had a little something to do with that.

As a result, without knowing it, my music expertise had clinched the part that I was there for, that of DJ Al Monte at the fictitious station, KRML. Clint had first wanted Flip Wilson to play the role, why I don't know, other than Flip was red hot at the time, hosting his own variety show. He was funny, telling jokes and coming out in drag as "Geraldine," screeching that Christopher Columbus was "gonna find Ray Charles." But when I heard about that, I said, to myself, "No way, honey. That ain't gonna happen! This role is mine!" And it was. I didn't even have to read for it. Clint later said he couldn't think of anyone who could have fit the part better. And he was right. Because I was Al Monte.

I was also cheaper than Flip. A lot cheaper.

Clint allowed me to put some flesh on the bone, pretty much writing my own lines, at least in the guise of being a DJ, which I did by fashioning Al Monte after the image of legendary DJ Magnificent Montague, using some of his expressions and exhortations. When I rehearsed, I'd say, "This is Sweet Al Monte," "sweet" being a big word on the street and in the barbershops where black guys met up. Clint loved it, but it caused a flutter when Clarice Taylor, the actress who played a character named Birdie, didn't like it. Clarice was in her mid-fifties at the time, and she was old school, a throwback to when blacks didn't preen or strut (she later played the grandmother Anna Huxtable on *The Cosby Show*). She was overruled, but she shunned me, and we never did hit it off. So be it. Realism was the essential element of *Play Misty for Me*. I'm real, man—that was the attitude I would project.

I had no time to waste. Shooting was to begin the next day, and when my scenes were filmed, I just started rattling off idiomatic DJ banter, none of it scripted. I don't even know if it made any sense; I made up all that stuff on the spot. But it flowed. It sounded like I'd been a DJ all my life—in fact, many viewers assumed I was a real DJ. My prattle was so compelling that Clint decided to use it as the opening scene. Al Monte is in the studio, vocally caressing the microphone:

"Hey, hey, you're digging the master jock for solid rock. . .. Sweet Al Monte blasting, babies. Being bold and pouring coal on KRML in quaint little Carmel-by-the-Sea. We're next door to magnificent Monterey, home of the annual jazz festival. Although it's four months away, you got to get your tickets, because they're going fast, and it can't last. The time is 7:54 and there's a breeze of 50 degrees around your loving hips, and there's a taste of fog. I say we got a bowl of soul, and if you think your heart can take it, come fly higher with The Heavy! Now we're gonna wrap it up for the week, folks. A brand-new release from the funk capital of the world, "Squeeze Me." Here he comes, the big "D" himself, Dave Garver. And Dave is gonna bring you five hours of mellow groove. In the meantime, this is Sweet Al Monte saying: Hang in there, babies, because everything is going to be everything. 'Bye."

Then, as a record plays, Al has the first interaction with Clint, who is reading a fan letter.

MONTE: What's that letter you got there? Is that that Frisco gig?

GARVER: Yeah.

MONTE: All right, so what's happening?

GARVER: They want the usual thing: a biography, pictures.

MONTE: Really? Is that that Madge Brenner chick?

SWING LOW, MY SWEET CHARIOT

GARVER: Yeah, she's the one putting it together.

MONTE: Well, in that case, David, you're in.

GARVER: How do you figure that?

MONTE: Now, David, come on, man. Are you kidding?

GARVER: Hey, she's a grandmother.

MONTE: Well, so when did that ever stop you? Hey, man, you better get a move on. I already played your theme.

GARVER: Yeah, I heard it. You're a real human being.

MONTE: And you're on the air, baby.

Clint tried to stay with me on the unscripted dialogue, but let's face it, Rowdy Yates ain't no Jimmy Mack. He was damn good, though, with the scripted lines, such as when Garver comes on the air, oozing, "Men have destroyed the roads of wonder, and their cities squat like black toads in the orchards of life. Nothing is clean, or real, or as a girl, naked to love, or to be a man with." Is it any wonder he has a stalker? Jessica makes her entrance moments later, or rather her voice does, as Evelyn Draper, when Dave takes a call:

GARVER: KRML, Dave Garver speaking.

DRAPER: Hello?

GARVER: Hi, what'll it be?

DRAPER: Play "Misty" for me.

Uh-oh. That's what everyone watching thought. Uh-oh. You could tell Garver was hooked. Uh-oh.

Remember, this was new territory for Clint, displaying a vulnerability that never surfaced even for a second in his stone-faced cowboy roles. He didn't even know if he had it in him, but he did, and we could see him mature right before our eyes. With his confidence growing, he began to accept deviations from the script, which was to my benefit because I always had ideas about how to make the script better. I was a natural-born troublemaker, so I gave it all I had, and Clint began making my part larger.

Clint came to use me as a kind of counterbalance, an instigator, always cool and clever. When Al drops in on Dave at his house, he spots the bronze statue of a nude woman. Al's eyes widen and he presses his hand against the statue's breast, cooing, "Solid silicone." It came out in jive, something like solid sillycone. Again, that was not in the script. Clint looked at me as if to say, "Where the hell did that come from?" He could barely keep from breaking up. But he knew it hit right. Same when he asks Al if he wants a beer. I don't just say no, as it's written in the script. Instead, I say, "I could go for something more uplifting, but not a brew, my man."

The rest of that scene, in which Al tries to get Garver to go out for dinner at a restaurant, goes on just like that, the two of us riffing back and forth, seeing who could top the other:

GARVER: Yeah, I know the joint, but I don't have a date, and I got a lot to do, really.

MONTE: Well, big deal, man. Get one! If you have any problems getting one, I'll get one for you as nice as I look.

GARVER: It's too late, and besides, I've got a lot of work to do.

MONTE: Hey man, but you gotta eat, David.

GARVER: I'm gonna whip up something here in my own kitchen.

MONTE: You know, David, I'm really worried about your social life.

GARVER: You know something? You're gonna make somebody a tremendous mother.

MONTE: Too narrow in the pelvis.

GARVER: I sure appreciate you dropping by, Al. Come by again sometime, anytime.

MONTE: Never let it be said that Sweet Al Monte can't take a hint.

That's when Evelyn— "that little 'Misty' chick"—shows up at his door.

We had a lot of fun with it, and the lighthearted dialogue served a purpose: It was meant as comic relief to the constant dread and anticipation of doom. Mine wasn't a big part, but it was an integral one. It set the tone in a lot of ways. That was why Clint let me get away with adding my own little touches. He was a hands-off director, anyway. Most of the scenes in that film were done in one take; Clint would like what he saw and say, "That's a wrap." He wouldn't go all day to get one scene right, partly because time was money.

Some of the experienced actors would say, "Wait, Clint, I can do it better. Let's try it again."

He would say, "No, we got it." They would brood that he wasn't letting them show their best work. But Clint had good judgment about the feel of a scene.

He also liked that I would always have a little surprise cooked up, such as when Al smokes dope in one scene. Now, this was a big deal back then. We were treading on dangerous ground. But I said, "This is about disc jockeys. Those guys smoke dope all the time." So, it went down that way. Audiences would get it by the way I held the cigarette in my hand, like a joint, pinching the smoking end while sticking my other three fingers up in the air and drawing the smoke into my poor lungs. I probably overacted in that scene to make the point, but it worked. But, wow, Universal went nuts over that. These days, it's nothing, even expected, but this was 1971, and movie studios were a decade or more behind the times. Clint fought to keep it in. To be honest, I didn't take the liberties I could have in that movie. I caused enough trouble.

Trouble was the word for making that movie. During the shooting, George Santoro, one of the execs at Universal, came up to Carmel, we heard, to pull the plug on the picture. The honchos at the studio had seen the rushes, and they believed it wasn't working and wasn't worth continuing. To them, a story about a crazy woman killer would turn off audiences. Plus, there was this black guy smoking dope. The truth was, just me doing that could have killed off one of the greatest suspense movies ever made! Fortunately, Clint was able to buy time to finish it, then we all drove down to L.A. for the editing phase. And that's where Clint saved it. He and the film editor made a rough cut, integrating the music and heightening the suspense, and Clint took it to a theater in Bakersfield for a test screening before an audience. When asked about their reactions to the movie, the audience members said things like "thrilling," "frightening," "scared out of my mind." There wasn't one negative comment, so Clint knew he had something special. He took the cut to Sid Sheinberg and, although the brass was still skeptical, they went ahead with the release.

Clint's frugality helped, too. He had brought it in for under $1 million, a real bargain for Universal, for which they were grateful—and more so when it made ten times that, at least, which streamed into the coffers of Universal and Malpaso—the rest of us peons, besides Jessica, who was the only other major actor in the movie, made union scale, with Clint reaching into his pocket to give us a few thousand more. Clint came out the big winner, of course, but so did Bob Daley, who would go on to produce every film made by Clint until 1985. As for me, I was being recognized on the street for the first time; people would call out, "Hey, Sweet Al!" That has stuck with me to this day. I was now firmly in the Clint Eastwood circle, to be called upon again down the road.

When I look back, *Play Misty for Me* was the most rewarding project I ever worked on; it was the stuff of legend (and incidentally, the best catered movie of any project). There was just something magical about how it all worked so well. Clint had already started thinking about doing a sequel when we scattered in different directions, and for me, the movie was a calling card. I was in eight or nine more films after *Misty*. I did two more with Clint, *Every Which Way but Loose* and *Sudden Impact*. We were going to do a third, the sequel to *Misty*, but the writer, Jo Heims, had passed away.

It was around that time that Jack Valenti, president of the Motion Picture Association, known then as the most powerful man in the industry, had a role for me to play in real life. In 1970, the FCC instituted the Primetime Access Rule, which prevented networks from having more than three hours a night on their local affiliates, to encourage local fare of community interest. It sounded noble, but it led to venerable "rural" series, like *The Beverly Hillbillies* and *Hee Haw*, being axed. Of course, the networks fought like hell against it (they would eventually get the rule repealed in 1996) and Jack, who was based in D.C., used his influence to arrange Congressional hearings on the rule in the mid-'70s. Knowing the other side would be led by the spellbinding Rev. Jesse Jackson, Jack wanted someone with as dramatic a flair. That turned out to be Yours Truly.

That performance helped usher me toward my ground-breaking role on *Tenafly*. I was fortunate enough to be the first African American to star in his own NBC TV crime drama series. Contrary to popular belief, Bill Cosby was not the first, although *I Spy* aired earlier, the series didn't star Cosby, he and Robert Culp were co-stars. *Tenafly* revolved around private detective Harry Tenafly, who in many ways lived like a white man, but happened to be black. Despite drawing an initial audience of over 30 million viewers in its debut, NBC elected not to renew the show after four episodes. Even I agreed with some critics that the show could have used more bite, more blackness, as it were. But even so, we had done something to be proud of. It was lauded by most. The New York Times named *Tenafly* as one of the top five new shows that season. And having a black man as the title character surely should have been a reason to sit up and take notice — and it was, but with the wrong people. In Texas, the local NBC affiliate ran the premier episode without sound for about fifteen or twenty minutes—an "accident" that was more likely sabotage. But what stuck in my craw was that the NAACP didn't say a word about the unfair cancellation. In 1974, Bill Lane, then-president of the Hollywood chapter of the NAACP, asked me to be a "distinguished presenter" at their annual Image Awards Show—in a letter that came exactly one day after the cancellation. I respectfully declined, noting the contrast of the NAACP's exuberant praise of *All in the Family* but saying nothing about a show portraying a smart black man with a loving family who didn't need to shoot it out with the bad guys to bring them in.

That's not to say I was above a role in *All in the Family*. In fact, I appeared twice on the show. I admit I am still tickled about the second episode, in which I play a black man named "Solomon Jackson," whose name Archie Bunker sees while looking for a token Jew for his racist lodge. He mistakenly assumes anyone with the name Solomon Jackson must be Jewish. Archie's shocked reaction when he sees Solomon in the flesh and realizes he has just recruited a black man is priceless. At that point, seeing through Archie's game, Solomon does a little jig and exclaims, "Hava nagila, y'all!" While I liked working with Carroll O'Connor and Norman Lear, I had a problem with the real-world consequences of a show that encouraged the racism it intended to skewer with parody.

When Hollywood seemed ready to tackle race issues head on, it was in the form of a miniseries, *Roots*, based on the bestselling book by Alex Haley. When the project was in the early stages of casting, it seemed that just about every black actor in town was asked to participate, including me. I was one of the few to turn it down. Despite the involvement of Alex Haley, I just was not interested in being part of what I assumed—correctly, I might add—would be a white man's drama about slavery. In 1977, *Roots* premiered to mostly favorable reviews as an eight-episode limited series on ABC. It garnered 37 Emmy nominations—to this day still the most nominations received by one show—and became part of the zeitgeist of America in the late 1970s. Not wanting to be left out in the cold, NBC soon after decided to make its own "Explosive Epic of the South" about plantation life and the evils of slavery. It was called *Beulah Land*, and the first of its three episodes aired on October 7, 1980.

I was hesitant to participate in this series, as well, but, to my everlasting regret, I somehow ended up in the role of a blacksmith named Ezra. When Ramsay King, casting director for the project, called me saying that Fred Silverman, then president of NBC and erstwhile producer of *Beulah Land*, wanted me to play a role in the miniseries, I explained my reasons for not wanting to participate: One, I had read the script and thought its portrayal of blacks was denigrating, and two, I thought Ossie Davis would be better suited to the role. Ramsay convinced me that the changes I wanted would be made to the script; after all, scripts are changed all the time. So, I accepted the role, assuming that the producers and directors would be willing to collaborate and listen to my ideas about how

I thought Ezra should be played. I was sorely mistaken. Fred was the producer, and his word was law. It so happened that Virg Vogel, the initial director, and I flew out to the location in Natchez, Mississippi, on the same flight, and it was then that I learned that Fred wouldn't allow any changes to the script.

In one scene, Ezra was supposed to stand and watch as his son was bullwhipped by Roscoe Corlay, the plantation owner, portrayed by Paul Shenar, for playing with his white son. I took objection to that. Producer Chris Morgan argued that an enslaved man would have likely been killed if he attempted to intervene in the whipping of his son, but for Ezra to just stand by and watch as his son was brutalized implied that black men were weak and cowardly, too afraid of punishment to protect their families. I asked him, "What kind of a man would not be willing to die to protect his son? Wouldn't you be willing to risk your life for your son? I damn sure would die for mine!" To me, it seemed obvious that the showrunners thought that was how an enslaved black man would—or should—react. I argued my case, Chris agreed to make changes, and we filmed the scene with Ezra taking the beating for his son. The next day, though, when I wasn't on set, they re-shot the scene with the boy being whipped and cut in a shot of my "reaction." I was so outraged that I later went public about my disgust with the series' depiction of stereotypical black characters, all of whom seemed perfectly content to be enslaved.

I was so sickened by *Beulah Land* and its portrayal of black people that I had my name removed from the credits of the series. I'm glad I did, too, because the show was not just panned but decimated by the critics. Tom Shales of *The Washington Post* begins his review, "'Beulah Land' is not suitable for human habitation." Joan Hanauer of United Press International writes, "'Beulah Land' has something in it to offend almost everybody, the people 'Beulah Land' is likely [to] insult in varying degrees include blacks, historians, Southerners whose families did not own great plantations, men in general, Yankees, and anyone of average intelligence." Despite the awful reception, *Beulah Land* did receive one Emmy nomination: Grady Hunt was nominated for costume design. In an irony that still causes me to shake my head, I—the one who stood alone in criticizing the piece -- who had spoken to the press about how terrible I thought the show was—was asked to represent *Beulah Land* at the awards show. Obviously, I did not hesitate in turning down that offer.

There were other opportunities though, that I turned down that turned out to be costly. I turned down roles in both *The Color Purple*, and *Star Trek: The Next Generation*, those parts ended up being filled by Danny Glover and Patrick Stewart. These decisions had something to do with a certain casting director, but I honestly don't regret missing out on those roles, and I would turn them down again if faced with the decision today. Acting is much like being an A&R man in the music business: You have to trust your gut. For whatever reason, those roles just weren't right for me at the time, and I'm glad that the actors who went on to fill them found success.

Luckily, my gut didn't say no when Dean Hargrove called me in the mid-'80's about portraying Lt. Brock in the new *Perry Mason* series he was doing. I needed the money, but I told him I was sick of the business, tired of fighting and the hypocrisy --but, because it was him, I would do one episode, maybe two. All told, I ended up doing eighteen *Perry Mason* made-for-TV movies. I liked working with Raymond Burr and Barbara Hale, and Dean is one of my best friends to this day, so the *Mason* set was one I enjoyed going back to. Raymond commanded a great deal of respect on the set, and people would defer to his judgement. Toward the end, when I believe Raymond knew he was dying, he teased me that in the last *Mason* movie we'd do together, his character would lose his first criminal case, defending none other than my character, Lt. Clifford Brock, on a murder charge! Unfortunately, Raymond passed away before we could work together again, and so Perry Mason's winning record remains intact (as a bit of trivia, the only two criminal cases that Perry Mason ever lost were overturned when Perry clears his defendants' names). As for Barbara Hale, she was a wonderful person with a great sense of humor, and we remained friends until her death in 2017.

Mason was filmed in Denver, Colorado and during the filming of one episode I decided that I would use some of my down time to rent a car and drive to the top of Pike's Peak. As I recall I rented a compact car and invited a friend to come along. Pike's Peak is one of the few mountains you can actually drive to the summit, but it's not an easy trek; the drive is 19 miles long and contains 156 turns and you ascend 6715 feet in those 19 miles. As I neared the top, I began to experience a dread that I had never felt before. It was frightening, I was imagining wolves - everywhere. The memory of all those wolves would be the basis of a book I would write some years later. *The Great Canus Lupus* would be the name, since it was the tale of the wily leader of a notorious wolf pack. The book was written completely tongue in cheek. Someone suggested I should make into a film. Things fell into place quickly, so quickly that I thought it would be a good idea to ask my good friend, Clint Eastwood to direct since it was a western. It would be filmed at the Pike's Peak locale. Ironically enough I had been in Colorado with Clint to film *Every Which Way but Loose*.

The book was well received. "This is a powerful tale, not since Jack London's *Tale of the Wild*, has an author so persuasively set forth the powerful world of animals, but McEachin does more than that. He has created a compelling fantasy, peopled by fascination characters, besides Blood, the alphas wolf, they include, JW MacBean, the sheepherder, who is the alpha wolf's sworn enemy, Steiner, the sheriff of a strange village - with off centered inhabitants, and Bud Blossom, a aging black cowboy who is the ironic voice of sanity in the most peculiar setting."

He continued, "It takes a confident author to stretch his talents towards a new and difficult goal. It takes a great author to achieve that goal. With *The Great Canus Lupus*, James McEachin proves himself to be a great American Author." I would like to thank my good friend, Will Ross, for that quote; unfortunately, the film was never made.

There was a point in time during the run of *Perry Mason* movies when Dean had the idea for a show about a southern lawyer, and when he took the idea to the network, they agreed to make a pilot. Dean had been looking for a way to work with Andy Griffith and was eager to offer him the role of Matlock, the old country lawyer who uses his guile and wit to exonerate his clients. The show was written for Andy, Linda Purl, Kene Holliday, and me. The only problem was that I really didn't want to do a television series, so I quit after eight episodes. They thought I was kidding. I was making good money; if I remember correctly, I was paid $40,000 for the pilot and $20,000 a week thereafter. I just didn't enjoy the demands of a series, though. It felt mundane to perform the same character all the time after my years of doing a variety of walk-on roles. Plus, Andy was quite a piece of work. I know that this isn't what you want to hear, because everyone loves

Andy Griffith, but he just wasn't that lovable kind of guy. He'd been a star too long and had to be in charge or he wasn't happy. He and Dean didn't get along—and everyone got along with Dean. Audiences, though, loved *Matlock*. To this day, when people meet me, they want to know about the time I spent working on that show. I honestly don't even think it was that they loved *Matlock* as much as they loved *The Andy Griffith Show*. Never underestimate the power of nostalgia.

I returned to the small screen in 2002 when I was offered the role of a Supreme Court Associate Justice in *First Monday*. It starred the late James Garner and Joe Mantegna. That show seemed to hit the right nails on the head; it was timely, the acting and scripts were generally good, and the production values were exceptional. But, like *Tenafly*, it could have been better. The critics didn't have too many nice things to say about *First Monday*, though Christine Corcos of the online journal *Picturing Justice* wrote of the show: "The one redeeming social value is the acting. The wonderful Charles Durning, who has bad limericks to recite, James Garner, Joe [Mantegna] and the much-underrated James McEachin are among the talented bunch trapped in this mess." Personally, I thought Jim Garner deserved an Emmy for his participation. It would have been a wonderful tribute to a guy who had had a nice career. He was never properly recognized. Perhaps it had something to do with the lawsuit he filed against Universal Studios for what he called "creative differences." Then, later on, I figured he must have been thinking "creative accounting,"—a pejorative term commonplace in Hollywood, meant to convey how studios are known to rip off even the best of actors. Garner boiled it down to the entertainment industry being "a bunch of greedy people." I, too, had problems with studio bosses, including the biggest network TV boss, Fred Silverman, and probably lost some roles because of it. Let's just stipulate that my stay in the acting profession wasn't built to last indefinitely. And it didn't.

With Harry Belafonte and Sidney Poitier on the set of Buck and the Preacher.

With Walter Matthau and Gene Kelly on the set of Hello Dolly.

Printed in U.S.A. ©Universal Pictures. Permission granted for newspaper and magazine reproduction only.

With Clint Eastwood and Jessica Walter on the set of Play Misty For Me.

On the set of Play Misty for Me

On the set of the Rockford Files with James Garner

Family Christmas 1971

CHAPTER 9

SWING LOW, SWEET CHARIOT

After more than three decades of working in Hollywood, the acting bug gave way to my new incarnation as an author. Unfortunately, my connections and experience in the movie industry didn't end up helping me much as a writer. *Tell Me A Tale*, my first solo effort, was originally written as a screenplay, and no less than Henry Fonda and Hal Holbrook were both eager to play the pivotal part of the slaveholder, Mr. Archy. Hal, who had won five Emmys and a Tony award, and with whom I had worked three times, said he would be "honored" to do it. But the film wasn't made, because producers wanted me to change the shock ending to a more palatable, i.e., conventional, resolution. This was the reaction of many to the conclusion of *Tell Me A Tale*. In the story, the protagonist, a black boy named Moses, takes vengeance on the few remaining whites of Red Springs, North Carolina.

Producers didn't like the notion of a black boy getting away with killing the four white men who had murdered his father and his beloved Uncle Benny. I refused to change the ending and proved yet again what I believe producer and casting director Renée Valente once said about me: "McEachin is his own worst enemy." I set about converting the script into a novel—with no changes to the ending. You've got to hold out for what you believe in. After all these years, I am still fighting to get *Tell Me A Tale* done as a motion picture.

Converting *Tale* into a novel allowed me to continue pouring my energy into writing. My own childhood provided the rich details of the novel. Moses is the young protagonist of *Tell Me A Tale*, but the story is really about James McEachin, because when I sat down to flesh out that character, I only needed to reference my own life, one molded by events and thoughts, both great and small, within a private, rural, and unchanging world. Like me, Moses came from across the tracks in the American South, raised in the highly prosaic town where I was born on May 20, 1930—Rennert, North Carolina. In the slow-beating heart of Robeson County, almost invisible in the southeastern quadrant of the state not far from the South Carolina border, it lay there, quite nearly a black hole.

In Rennert, and sometimes in lonely little Red Springs the only cool breeze on blisteringly hot summer days while picking cotton— is the one in one's imagination. It was an activity that occupied a bit of my time when I was just a tyke. It still serves as a common occupation for black men there to support their families. In this context, Rennert can be seen as a vestige of the antebellum South, the phantoms of human bondage still palpable. However, I do not know if I descended from slaves, or if there were any slaves at all in Rennert. In my youth, as now, there were only around 200, mostly black residents of less-than-modest means battling to survive the Great Depression. I would call the place devoid of activity. To get to the "big town" you would need to go to Lumberton, a real-life version of Mount Pilot, the fictitious town in North Carolina that the folks in Mayberry considered the big town in *The Andy Griffith Show* back in the '60s.

Of course, poor black folks rarely make it into works of literature— something I wanted to remedy in *Tell Me A Tale*. The characters of my childhood were perfect for my purposes, as they inhabited a world in which time seemed to stand still. I can remember as if it were yesterday what was inside Mr. Archy's old shack, such that I could describe it precisely in *Tell Me A Tale* when describing Uncle Benny's kitchen. It was, I wrote:

"the center of activity. And the color of the dirt was red. It said it all. It was the utter depths of poverty. With its stained floor giving way to an old Thatcher stove whose chimney nervously touched a roof that was independent of anything secure, it almost defied description. The walls had never warmed to wallpaper, paint, or varnish, and the shelves that housed the few cooking and eating utensils sagged to U-bolt proportions. In the corner nearest the stove was a pile of chopped wood, and in the far corner there was a tub that represented a sink. In the center of the room was a homemade table with two weak chairs, and there was nothing else. Swinging into the adjacent room, the bedroom, there was a huge, high-posted wooden bed that suffered from age and was covered by a multicolored and multi soiled quilt that, despite its many colors, failed in the attempt to match anything. Diagonally across from the bed was a large trunk and next to it a bottom-hanging, high-backed rocking chair that angled away from the loose-bricked fireplace. A lone kerosene lamp nested on a small round table just a few feet forward of the front wall and flanking window. All over the tiny room, including the ceiling, there were faded patches of burlap, paper, and straw jammed in a host of cracks and crevices."

After the completion of *Tell Me A Tale*, I continued to draw on personal experiences as inspiration for my writing. I wrote *Farewell to the Mockingbirds*, the tragic story of the revolt by members of King Company, 3rd Battalion, 24th Infantry Regiment, when it was segregated during World War I. It was a revolt that was not much different than the street scenes I would see in Minneapolis a century later. Those men were me by other names. Sadly, those "mockingbirds" are as relevant as ever: The soldiers had been baited into their carnage by white cops. It was a human tragedy, one that need not have happened, yet similar tragedies continue to occur, as evidenced by the death of George Floyd and so many other black men and women.

There were no heroes but plenty of villains in the 24th's march on Houston. But from my perspective, the conditions—and the unreconstructed heritage of the Confederacy—made it inevitable, an irrational dynamic and sudden impulse. Those soldiers in Houston were similarly swept up by forces far beyond them, rooted in the virus of racism. Not deserving of sympathy but understanding. I made the point of getting inside the head of the pivotal character of First Sergeant Obie O. McClellan, one of the ill-fated soldiers. McClellan, I wrote:

"had always felt there was equality in war. In war, he believed, there was progress; blacks would be appreciated and would contribute on an equal footing…. Being accepted as loyal, in time of war, as wonderful as it was, did little to dispel the Army's long-held belief that the blacks didn't have the courage to fight [and were] indifferent and lazy. Nor did it eliminate the long-held beliefs that blacks were close to being freaks of nature and, as such, had no will or reason to fight. He, like all the others, had heard over and over again that war is noble and heroic, traits that surely could not be attributed to a race that had no pride in country or self. There was only one thing that could create a wholesale change to America—war."

These thoughts were a long way from being formed inside my mind and sense of justice while I was in the Army, given that I had few such thoughts at seventeen. But many years later when I wrote *Farewell*, I was able to draw on my own sense of unease and meld it with that of the soldiers themselves to draft those thoughts ascribed to McClellan.

My writings defy facile assumptions. Reviewers of my books have favorably cited the unorthodox plot lines and resolutions that are not the norm for literature dealing with racial evolution and attendant assumptions, including methods of justice-taking that might seem vigilantism on par with the barbarism of slavery and the hanging tree. In 2008, an extraordinarily bright and dedicated graduate student named Jennifer Loomis stunned me by writing a thesis contrasting *Tell Me A Tale* with Harriet Beecher Stowe's *Uncle Tom's Cabin* and Octavia E. Butler's *Kindred*. Her premise was that of a new "moral law within" arising in the work of the postmodern black literati, as opposed to the conventionality of *Tom's Cabin*, which of course has been read in schools for decades. Loomis writes, "McEachin pushes white readers to reconsider the stories that they have told and continue to tell about themselves and their past. Moreover, "he insists that white Americans must begin . . . to 'tell the truth' and that refusing to do so will have ethical consequences for the whole country." I do agree with Loomis' thesis. It was not a conscious intent, but her last line is spot on: "Americans, McEachin insists, must learn to tell a new tale." Amen to that.

When I sat down to start this memoir—which in itself was a journey of challenges—I didn't realize that reliving the circumstances of that journey, and most centrally my literary efforts later in life, would provide some important clues to my self-examination. As I reread the solitary thoughts of Moses, as he is on his way back home to North Carolina to kill his family's oppressors, I found these words resonating with me: "A better fate." That's exactly what he meant. A better fate. Those three little words had been almost an anthem in his young life. But along with it was the word deserving. *Not deserve—but deserving.* How apt, he always thought. How appropriate. How belonging. How them. How deserving. "Deserving," he always concluded, belonged right up there with the Ten Commandments. Moses himself would have approved.

The point there is, what, exactly, are we deserving of? This conundrum runs through my writings and through my head, prompting me to write of my life's meanderings. I still had not learned enough about my own life, the fruits of my own journey, bitter and sweet and bittersweet, until I had to confront the scary vagaries of writing an autobiography. And while I envisioned this work as a book of life—of my life—the content takes the form of reliving several lives.

My hope is that I have helped to reshape the way that Americans tell stories about race, and that books like *The Heroin Factor*, *Say Goodnight to the Boys in Blue*, *The Great Canis Lupus*, and *Pebbles in the Roadway* have helped to redraw the role, reach, and importance of the black writer. I can feel my racial pride down to the marrow when one of our literary giants brands my work as authentic. One of the most prized possessions in my cluttered office is a card I received in 1989 from Maya Angelou, citing my "sumptuous and consistently grand" work. I cannot begin to describe the exhilaration that sweeps over me when a literary critic of stature writes that my use of colloquial, idiomatic vernacular and dialogue makes it seem as though one can see and feel a scene as one reads it. If so, I can only say this is a God-given gift.

The more I wrote, the more I realized that writing provided considerably more clarity and purpose to my daily existence as well as an avenue for exploring my life experiences. It was through my writing that I began to process and understand in a new light my childhood poverty, my near-death experiences, and even my good fortune in the music and film industries.

Then, as if waiting for this metamorphosis, my military service was finally recognized. Although I had been awarded the Purple Heart in 1953, my service records were destroyed in a fire where military files were kept. For fifty-two years, there was no official record of my service. Finding the records became a detective story, information would trickle in bit by bit from many sources. It took until 2002 for my records to be recovered, leading to the awarding of another medal I considered undeserved, the precious Silver Star, as well as seven medals of valor. Since then, I have been bestowed several commendations by state legislatures. Thanks to the tireless work of one of the finest men I've ever met, Tiger Davis, a delegate in the Maryland legislature and a professor at Morgan State University, I was given the school's Distinguished Achievement Award on the 50th anniversary of the Korean War's end. I have even been honored by the legislature of Mississippi.

I still find it breathtaking.

I was scheduled to give a speech at the 2008 Republican Convention, but it was canceled when things ran long. As I waited to go on backstage, I caught a glimpse of Senator John McCain, who would accept the nomination for president that night. He had a way of making people feel they were his friends. He was a man of high honor, rectitude, spirit, yet he could not lift his arm to salute the flag, his arm having been mangled during his years spent in a North Vietnamese prison. And here I was, a comrade in arms, metal fragments from bullets still lodged in my stomach, between my ribs, and in my leg, still causing pain at times. But we were both survivors, he at the pinnacle of his life, and I felt the joy he was feeling.

I am still trying to answer the question, "What are we deserving of?" For many years after Korea, I felt like a man stripped of his past. I didn't feel I'd done much to earn the Purple Heart and the Silver Star, at least not based on my fragmented memory of that time. Indeed, I felt I deserved no medals: Medals are for the heroes, and I wasn't heroic. I was injured without firing a shot, meaning I hadn't done the job. The other guys who lost their lives in that ambush deserved all their medals; they did far more than I did. I can still hear them firing. The prisoner who was hanging naked upside down as if on a meat hook, who never made it back either, deserved his. Years later, I was told that Lieutenant Schenk's medals, which had been lost, had been found by a patriotic young woman from North Carolina who had bought some items at a yard sale. Kimberly Paller saw Lt. Schenk's name on the Purple Heart and wanted to return it to its rightful owner. She traced the name back to our 2nd Infantry Division, and through her perseverance, she somehow found a way to contact me to see if I could find his family and return the medal to them. It became my obsession, because it was Lt. Henry Schenk whose life needed to be cherished and enshrined. Major Zachariah Fike will have my everlasting gratitude, as he and Purple Hearts Reunited were able to lend invaluable assistance to me in seeing that Henry Schenk's family receive his medals at a ceremony in Washington, D.C.

Though the government gave back my past, they can never give me back those years. For others, black men who are contemporaries of mine, who fought with me, who died next to me, they will never get their due. It is for all those men that I continue to remind my fellow Americans that the freedom we have today has not come easily, nor cheaply. Much of my work over the past twenty years has been dedicated to veterans, including the audiobook *Voices: A Tribute to the American Veteran* (winner of the Benjamin Franklin Award) and the short film *Reveille*. I returned to acting for the latter, which was a wonderful concept: no dialogue, only me and David Huddleston, who had co-starred with me on *Tenafly*. We are alone in the film, with each other and our memories, as we go through the routine of saluting the flag; both of us veterans, he Navy, me Army. It was first shown to the troops in Afghanistan and the reception— hard-bitten soldiers could not keep from openly weeping—told me I had struck the right chord. That showing in Afghanistan led to it being shown at the GI Film Festival in Washington, D.C. Adam and Donovan Montierth were the very capable producers of the film. It was posted on YouTube and received millions of hits. *Reveille* spawned the equally hushed *Old Glory*, also co-starring David. I had merely acted in the former, but for the latter I also wrote, produced, and directed, taking my aging vet character back on a sentimental journey through his past as a soldier in order to give a final salute to the landmarks and symbols of his service. I identified completely with my old soldier. At age 77, it also marked my directorial debut.

In 2017, I tried my hand at another screenplay with the semi-fictionalized *Until the Last Dog Dies*. I made it into a film short, and I was down to my last nickel, so to speak. But I had to do something, and I recalled Shakespeare's brilliant metaphor in *Julius Caesar* for the horror of combat: "Cry 'Havoc,' and let slip the dogs of war . . ." The script gave voice to my own conscience as a virtual character, leading my alter ego "James" back through his wartime hell and challenging his restiveness, which had provoked two failed suicide attempts. Very thankfully, it had never gotten quite that bad for me. I had wrestled with my devils, for sure, but never have I felt the need for expiation, in no way to the degree of ending my life. Even so, I could slip into the mind of my alter ego, who had pointed a gun to his temple—twice—each time putting a bullet into a wall instead of his head, as if the hand of God had overridden his own. I took this literary detour mainly as a way of humanizing post-traumatic stress disorder in veterans, because for them, it regularly does get that bad. For them, and this is the dirty little secret of veterans' issues, suicide is an option too often taken. But on a primal level, I was really speaking to myself, as a warning, and as a means of finding the way through the bramble of life. In the script, my conscience tells me:

'You were once a soldier, a policeman; a fireman, even—yet you couldn't hit a target—your temple—only inches away from the barrel of a gun you own. For years you have entertained the thought—and I dare say that lately you've been hell-bent on exercising the thought of "termination". Under the guise of what they say is acceptably suicidal. Nonsense. Yes, you've been hammered in life; yes, you've been driven by demons and such. But what gives you the right to go out and play God—to issue your own death warrant? Only God is God. In its truest form, the act of suicide is an act of repulsion that guarantees nothing in life, even less in the afterlife. I implore you to go back to serving that which has guided you through all your days and your nights; all of your nights. And your days…Go with him, James. Be with God."

The hand of God was there. No one knew that more than I. Every mile, every inch of this still-active journey has been guided from above by some- thing much more discerning than me.

In every way, my life has been a blessing. I have been watched over by God and His band of angels through every stage of my life. They were there when the doctors at the whites-only hospital in Robeson County saved me as a child. The angels prevented me from pulling the trigger on the blond-haired boy and gave him the physical and moral strength to drag me on that long and torturous journey from the creek to the relative safety of our outpost. They may have had a hand in helping me to succeed in the music business—despite having no earthly idea what I was doing—and the angels may have been responsible for Art Names walking up to me on the street to offer me a movie role that would lead to a decades-long career in acting. My life has followed a trajectory for which I can find little explanation, unless I accept that I have been prodded—and sometimes pushed—by something larger than me. Without the band of angels that has saved my life, both literally and figuratively, over and over, this story would be a lot different and, likely, a lot shorter. And while I am still wringing every drop of living from my days, I hope that when I arrive at the next destination on my journey, I will be reunited with all those whom I had come to love and admire during my time on Earth: Grandmother Becky, my mother, the friends I lost in Korea, Otis Redding, John Wayne, Barbra Hale, Raymond Burr. My dearly beloved Lois. Maybe I will finally be able to thank her for all she went through. Maybe Lt. Henry Schenk, who went down firing, and then there was the blond-haired boy. And lastly, leave a note for the children who never understood.

I hope those familiar faces who have crossed over will be waiting for me when my band of angels saves me again, this time swinging low their chariot to carry me home.

SAN DIEGO PADRES

Padres FIRST PITCH / AUGUST 24, 2005

With Wayne Newton

With Ed McMahon

"McEachin is the best actor I've ever known, and I've been in the entertainment business 39 years." --Tony Orlando, Entertainer

Kent Twitchell adding James to the "We the People: Out of Many, One" mural at the Bob Hope Patriotic Hall in Los Angeles

With Bill Clinton

With Ed Anser

Cast of First Monday
(Back Row) Joe Mantegna, James McEachin, Gail Strickland, Stephen Markle.
Front Row) Camille Saviola, James Karen, James Garner, Charles Durning, Lyman Ward.

With Michael Steele

Mrs. Audie Murphy

With Bob Dole

With John McCain

Congressman Dreier awards *McEachin the Silver Star*

ACKNOWLEDGMENTS

First, I would like to offer my gratitude to General Vincent Brooks for his gracious willingness to pen the Foreword to this book. Nobody can touch him. He is an unmitigated giant. He leads by foresight, he made West Point history when he became the first African American to be appointed to the highest position a cadet can hold, that of Cadet Brigade Commander. When the general was awarded his fourth star, he became only the eighth African American in the history of the U.S. military to earn this honor. During his 37 years of service, General Brooks interacted with 83 militaries from countries around the world. I am in awe of this great man and am touched beyond measure to have him say a few words about my memoir.

Judge Will Ross has been a friend and been through too many highs and lows for too many years to count since we met through another good friend, the late David Charnay.

Jennifer Loomis helped to revise and edit the book initially. Thank you to Mark Ribowsky for his writing contributions during the initial stages of the project and to Hazel Cox.

Connie Martin has been my trusted assistant for many years, and I would like to thank her for her long-standing support and friendship. Sometimes in the quiet of night all you need is someone to listen.

Thank you to my dear friends Robbie and Gary Delson, Congressman David Dreier, Doug LaViolette, Gary Sinise, Aaron Vessup, Jon Voight, Ed Asner, and Billy Bush. In one way or another these individuals have had an impact on my life for many years, and I am incredibly grateful for their willingness to listen and for their generosity, kindness, and patience.

Thank you to Kent Twitchell for including me in your historic mural. I also want to thank Lt. General Carol Mutter for her service and for being an inspiration to military women everywhere.

In thinking about the military there have been many extended hands that have helped along the way. They have shown appreciation for all that I have done promoting the veteran, from speaking before the Medal of Honor Society on Wall Street, the Military Order of the Heart, debuting my play at the Kennedy Center in Washington, D.C., or speaking at the National Cathedral. It is not possible to list everyone or everything or every organization by name, but some of these people who know what pain is were immensely helpful and I would sure like to extend a heartfelt thank you to the friends, neighbors, doctors, nurses, and veterans who have popped by and/or gave me a thumbs up in one way or another. I thank you all.

Thank you to my dear friend since childhood, Eugene Marshall, who passed away just as I was finishing this book. Something told me to move on. And I did.

Before writing the *finis* to this journey, allow me to submit a few additional pieces. The first, entitled WAR, could be classified as a substantial piece that I wrote as a speech, venting my feelings about mankind's greatest tragedy – man's inhumanity to man. I had recently been appointed as an US Army Reserve Ambassador, a position which carried with it the protocol rank of Major General. Not bad for an ex-Staff Sergeant. I was proud to have the opportunity to serve once again.

ADDENDUM A

WAR
THE OLD SOLDIER SPEAKS ON WAR

We are told by archeologists that man has been on earth for 125,000 years. We, as a young country, can take little comfort in the knowledge that we have been here for considerably less than 250 years and already we have been involved in more than a hundred wars, deployments and skirmishes. We have done so in the name of liberty. Our military has seen the service of more than 42 million people since the inauguration of that first Continental Army in 1775. Since that time, the military has seen 651,000 battle deaths, one and one half million wounded, and thousands and thousands more listed as missing in action. Today, there are more than twenty-six million veterans listed on the national roster.

War is unquestionably a filthy business; it is a life-taking business. In the early 1800s, Karl von Clausewitz, the quintessential theorist on the subject of War, observed: "Politics is the womb in which war develops." Owing to the notion that the world has been politicized since the dawn of man, and coupling this thought with the chilling observation made by one of history's more tyrannical leaders, Mao Tse-tung, former Chairman of the Communist party -- and one who advanced the thought: "War can only be abolished through war, and that in order to get rid of the gun it is necessary to pick up the gun," -- it seems likely that man will know war for as long as man inhabits

Earth.

Today, with religion at the core, and this hateful new thing called terrorism at the reins, we are engaged in one of history's more peculiar wars. With all of our sophistication, modern weaponry, and technologies, we are, in the main, back to where man started: reconnoitering mountains and fighting in caves.

To quote Benjamin Franklin, there never was "a good war or a bad peace." It is a dilemma that plagues this nation on a daily basis – and whether one's politics is for this war or against this war, the issue exists as to whether this nation is to stoop to the level of an anemic enemy who has mislaid the values of religion and has allowed perversion and fanaticism to be his rule; or whether we are to take a more stand-strong posture and use increased might in defending the principals that we have clung to since birth.

In the interest of humanity, we will do as we have done in wars past. We will continue to choose restraint. But this crazed new force, emboldened by that choice, will continue to misconstrue restraint for weakness; thus, our homeland and the entire Western World will be under threat for years to come. And even if we were to concede all that we have, and all that we stand for to this enemy, still we will be under threat; for his is a force impossible to satisfy.

And so, it has become necessary to bid farewell to the peace and tranquility we have known for so long in America. Ours now is to prepare for seasons upon seasons of discontent. It does not mean surrender or capitulation to evil; rather it is the altering of a way of life in the sobering realization that the tentacles of war have touched us as nothing has ever touched us before.

God has bestowed many blessings on us in these United States. Freedom is foremost among them -- and this is what so disturbs this new enemy of ours: Freedom -- that precious gift of self-determination. In this land of bounty and beauty you can be what you want to be; but the best one can be, always, is to be an American.

It disturbs this new enemy to know that we are not a nation of infidels, driven by greed and commerce. We are, at times, frivolous --

brash and sassy, we are sometimes given to audaciousness and overconfidence and jingoism, -- but principally, we are a nation of fidelity and purpose, with a deep and abiding concern for our fellow man. We are an exuberant people, a resilient people of pride and hope. We have tried, at all times, to keep our eyes on the broad expanse of the universe; and we have tried, in all ways, to share our blessings with those in need. We Americans are an optimistic people -- and it is that optimism that causes us to believe in the ultimate rise of the human spirit. But being neither purveyors of truth nor devotees of the good, this new enemy would like the world to think that we are a hypocritical, crass, and intrusive people, forcing shallowness and superficiality on the gullible and unsuspecting; that these United States is a bastion of corruption and immorality -- that it is the home of the great Satan, cradle of all things repugnant and irreligious.

This new enemy would like the world to think that we are led by an imperiously arrogant government; that, by design, it is a machine of war, bent on imposing dominance over a weak and naïve world. They choose to ignore the fact that this government is a freely elected government; that it represents the will of the people, and like the people, it remains rooted in hope and conviction; that this young country, with all of its faults and missteps in growing, has, in its short history, done more for mankind than they -- or any other nation -- has done in all of their centuries of existence, and that the nation does not exist whose lot has not been aided by America's generosity. Name a world-wide catastrophe that has occurred in our day and age, and you've named a place where the helping hand of America has been. This nation has been responsible for the liberation of over a billion people; we have fed and sheltered millions, and no one has benefited more from our humanitarian efforts than our former enemies.

True, we have fought in many wars -- even amongst ourselves, but our aim has always been for peace. And, failing in the effort to secure the peace, we have tried to fight with honor. And when war was over and the guns silenced, we have always managed to find a way to supplant aggression with compassion, and skilled though we were in war, there were no finer ambassadors of peace and goodwill; no better emissaries of a great and giving nation than those who donned the uniform and fought our battles.

It is those qualities we continually seek to share with all mankind.

We make neither pretense nor excuse for our strength and position in a vastly troubled world. We are a power, in the interest of the dictates of freedom, we must remain a power. Rightly or wrongly, we are able to say to those who have taken action against us -- to say to those who contemplate taking action against us: "We have enough weapons of mass destruction to level you and all that is yours." But this nation will never -- ever -- utter the words, for ours is not to destroy. Ours is for peace -- for unity, for the dignity of the human race.

We seek to say to all: "Ours is not to subvert your will of honor, take your land, subjugate your people, or interfere with your sacred pursuits. This America is a God-fearing America, but you are entitled to believe in whomever -- or whatever -- you choose. We desire, only, that you lay down your sword and shield -- and come... sit at the table of brotherhood. And, together, through our individual interpretations, we will find a way to harken to the words of an old song, wherein it is said: 'I ain't gonna study war no more.'"

For peace and unity -- for the sake of the universe, it takes no more than that.

Grand Marshall at the Memorial Day Parade in Washington, DC

ADDENDUM B

STARS

THE OLD SOLDIER SPEAKS ON LOVE

I saw her as she was coming down the gangplank. And I said to myself her war, like many wars before, was behind her. With a chest full of medals, she was back in the United States, and, after an extended stay in the military, she will be on her way home. She was proud, but uneasy. Occupying her mind was that day, many years ago, when, as a little girl she had left school and she was not feeling very well. Normally – that is, if she hadn't had an encounter on the playground -- she would be running and skipping – feeling bouncier and freer than all the colors of spring. But on that long-ago day she had sauntered home. She was feeling a bit wobbly – woozy, as children say. But there was a reason: she was nursing a black eye -- and, occasionally – she was seeing dizzying, cascading stars, colliding under a puffy eyelid. But bravely, there would be no tears.

When she arrived home, she curled up on the front-porch swing. As a test, she tried to bring into clear focus the picket-fence that tried to shelter a yard of colorful flowers that she loved so much. But it seemed as if the swing conspired against her, and it became all the more upsetting because, in its unsteadiness, it managed to give lightheaded movement to both the fence and the yard, and so she stood again and tried to collect herself in other ways. But that, too, had its moments; and so, she mustered courage and went inside.

Her head was hanging just a little bit lower, and she was still seeing -- and feeling -- those dizzying, by-passing stars when she nestled close to the back of her father's big chair there in the living room.

But she really didn't have to get close. The man with the kind eyes and wise face already knew. He had already laid his paper aside; he was standing when his precious little girl entered the room. Saying nothing, he knelt down, looked at her darkened eye, touched her face gently, and stroked her pigtails for a moment. Then he put a comforting arm around her, and said, "Honey; do you remember what your dad said about not fighting?"

"Yes, sir," she said, softly, and still not permitting the tears to come.

With more gentle patience, he said, "We've talked about this fighting thing several times before, haven't we?"

She nodded slowly. "Yes, sir,"

He studied her delicate face again, kissed her softly on the cheek, and continued with fatherly guidance, "You see, sweetheart, we talk about these things because your dad is a man of peace. And your dad would like for you to grow up and become a symbol of peace. There's too much fighting in this world of ours, and we gain little or nothing by it. And little girls – little girls shouldn't even think of fighting. To begin with, it's unladylike. And you are a little lady. But even if you were a little boy, you shouldn't fight. Little boys shouldn't fight; big boys shouldn't fight; even big people – even this present war, we shouldn't be involved in it. Fighting of any kind is wrong. And as soon as this country comes to its senses and puts a stop to it, the better off we'll all be. – Now, look at me and promise: no more fighting. Okay?"

The good eye wandered around the room, came back, and landed on him. And thoughtfully she asked, "Dad; don't fight? -- even if it's some- thing worth fighting for?"

"Even if it's something worth fighting for, "dear heart. "There's always compromise, my darling... always compromise -- Remember when I talked to you about the meaning of compromise?"

"Yes, sir," she said, quietly.

"Well, dear heart, it's something I really want you to remember. And practice."

"I will, sir," she said. "I will."

"– Now," he said, "Tell me, how did you get the black eye?"

She became almost breathless. Sending the dizzying, by-passing stars off to recess, she started talking with urgency. "It was almost the same as before, Sir. But only this time we were on the playground, and another boy called you a coward because you didn't go to the war and fight like his father did. I told him the same as I told the other boys before -- that you're a peaceful man, and you didn't believe in fighting. Nobody should fight, I said. And he said he still didn't like you, Dad. And he called you another name. And he had done it before, Dad. He was one of the same boys who called you a coward before. But when he said it that time, I hauled off and socked him! I socked him real good, too!!"

"I bet you did; honey," said her farther. "But this time, the boy blackened your eye. Sweetheart, I hate to say this but maybe... just maybe this will teach you a lesson about fighting."

"But I didn't fight this time, Dad. I didn't fight. I popped him one time – in the nose. But I didn't fight. I promise, I didn't. I promise, I promise I didn't fight."

"Then, sweetheart," he said. "if you didn't fight, how did you get the black eye?"

Now holding back a new push for tears from both the good eyelid and the bad eyelid, she sniffed, "I did what you said, sir."

"And what was that?"

"I compromised."

"But my dear little girl; if you popped him in the nose, and he hit you in the eye -- where was the compromise?"

"Dad..." she said. "I wanted to pop him in his big fat mouth."

...Oh, how time has flown and things have changed through the years, she said to herself as she stood there looking over the place that seemed to have grown smaller over the years.

Now all grown up, she was coming home, not from school -- but from the military. She was coming home from war – and with a chest full of medals, no less.

She was uncertain and hesitant as she moved past the picket fence, now casting small, measured shadows over a deadened yard where flowers as colorful as her medals and ribbons once grew.

But there, on the porch, standing next to the swing that looked as though it hadn't seen true motion since she'd left, was her father – the peaceable man. She became frozen in that long-ago moment when he'd said he wanted her to grow up and be ladylike -- and to become a symbol of peace.

Neither of them moved or said anything for a long while, and then slowly he shuffled off the porch for a closer look at his daughter. He stood there studying her, her medals, and that spanking white dress uniform... and then he grabbed her – he grabbed her and he wouldn't let go; and he kept on repeating how proud he was of her. And then in a broken voice, he said, "My little girl... you are my hero." And the moment he said it, once again she saw stars – not the dizzying stars of old, but stars of a different kind; stars of warmth and love... And hope.

As for me, I am tired after being on the long and weary road. But soon the wheels of the carriage will be coming to yet another stop, as they will do all through eternity. But I will not be aboard the carriage this time, I will remain here at my new home -- remembering well what my grandmother used to say: home is where the heart is. My heart, my dear friends, continues to be with my military brothers and sisters -- and please note I have recently become involved with a very honorable organization: the Coalition of Families of Korean Cold War Veterans -- POWs and MIAs. They number in the thousands, and I am here to assure you, with your help, those who sacrificed their all will not be forgotten. As i said at a similar ceremony not too long ago ... And I am going to recite it at every opportune moment....

"On days of remembrances past --

ADDENDUM C

A story about Roosevelt "Jack" Clark, an American soldier, brought to our attention by Steven Mayer, a columnist for The Bakersfield Californian dateline March 1, 2013.

Missing for Six Decades, Local Soldier Finally Laid to Rest

What would Roosevelt "Jack" Clark had said if he were alive to see it? It is also a question I would pose to the young.

Hundreds of Bakersfield High School students, including scores of Junior ROTC cadets, lined the streets around the campus Friday as the funeral procession carrying Clark's remains passed by his alma mater. Escorted by Bakersfield police motorcycle officers and members of the Patriot Guard Riders, the motorcade elicited a respectful silence from the students.

"I'm glad for his family that he's finally made it back home where he belongs," said Desmon McGhee, 16, a technical sergeant with the Air Force Junior ROTC.

Calling the event, a "teachable moment," BHS Principal David Reese invited students to come out of their classrooms to show their respect to the deceased soldier and his family.

We're always talking about the Driller family," Reese said. "Part of that is remembering those who came before you."

Pfc. Clark grew up in Arvin and played for the 1949 Drillers football team, He was reported missing in action in late November 1950, while fighting with the 24th Infantry in North Korea. He was 18. And nearly 62 years passed with little word. Clark was declared dead, and members of his extended family began to accept the possibility that their loved one's remains might never be found or identified.

But at Friday's funeral service held at People's Missionary Baptist Church in southeast Bakersfield, Rosa Rentie, one of Clark's first cousins, recalled receiving a call from the Army five or six years ago. They wanted DNA samples from Rentie and her mother in hopes of identifying remains handed over by North Korea years before.

"She died a few months before we got the notification that they had identified his remains," Rentie said of her mom.

The church welcomed an estimated 200 to 300 mourners, black, white, Hispanic, Asian -- they came to pay their respects to a man who left home at age 18 and finally returned more than six decades later.

Veteran film and television actor James McEachin, who turned to writing in his later years, spoke at Friday's service, drawing a standing ovation at the conclusion of his remarks, a rarity at a funeral.

The poetry in his words was that powerful.

"On days of remembrances past, I have borne in mind that last full measure of devotion of which Abraham Lincoln so eloquently spoke at Gettysburg."

"From shadowed lanes, from far-away roads, I have looked off and seen the symmetrical obedience of numberless headstones that stand like dwarfed sentries for the honored dead. Often, I have thought of those buried at sea, and I have thought, too, of those interred in graves around the globe. They number in the thousands, and I do believe I can hear them crying out to each and every one of us, saying: I want to come home. I want to come home…" Oh, I say to you, Mr. and Mrs. America; I say to your sons and daughters; your young, your old, your rich, your poor; I say to all who are privileged to be within these borders, one cannot help but be touched by the price of our liberties, humbled by graves that stretch from coast to coast. On this day of tribute and remembrance, 'lo a day backed by the trembling winds of yet another war, strident voices of doubt and dissent have pushed me to a place beyond the site of graves and I find myself moving along stark, sobering corridors, dedicated to the living who have sacrificed much for democracies cause, I find myself in a hospice for the American veteran. Here I am swept amid remnants of wars old and new, the sorrowing consequence of battle ever so evident, I pray -- Oh, how I pray there never again be this need for war; but if, in the final hour, war we must, let it be for the principles for which our fathers stood, for the freedoms for which this God- anointed nation has been ordained to stand. Then when in observance of the toll of war or whether in ceremony of the great gifts of freedom, such as we now share, it is to those strident voices of doubt and dissent to whom I shall first look. I will pray to my God that we come together – even, that we unite as one –and over and over and over and over again, we give thanks –to the American veteran, defenders of freedom. And holding dear the memory of the dead and unaccounted for, I shall further pray that none among us forget those whom I see here in this place and in walks and hospices the country over – those who once stood tall for democracy, for the precious right to speak and assemble freely, but are now infirmly moving – without grace, down the long, long corridors of duty honor and sacrifice– going their separate way, silent of deed and sacrifice, yet ever and ever, they are still giving still giving their all to say to us all: No veterans, No Democracy, No America.

McEachin told the gathering that he enlisted in "that same segregated Army" that Clark was a part of, and he entreated all Americans to remember and honor Clark and all those who have served, living or dead -- for without them we would be lost.

Not everyone who wanted to attend Clark's memorial service was able to. Bakersfield resident Neal Vance planned to be at Clark's funeral, but health issues prevented his attendance. Vance said he's had a hard time sleeping since he learned that the remains of a comrade had been identified. Although Vance didn't know Clark, the coincidences between their lives make him feel like he did.

At age 80, Vance is the same age Clark would be had he survived. Like

Clark, Vance went to Bakersfield High, left school early to join the Army and was sent to combat duty in Korea. And both men were in the snow and below-zero cold of North Korea when Chinese troops unexpectedly entered the war, devastating American lines in an extended battle that would change the course of the war.

"It was a lousy day," Vance said in obvious understatement. "Clark went through hell that day. I'm sure he did," Vance said. "But now he's home for good."

Beyond the Call
(Photo Credit 14106203 / James Mceachin © Candace Beckwith | Dreamstime.com)

ADDENDUM D

The genesis of this story began in the quiet of a late summer's day. To me, it is more about grit and determination than anything else. But please don't question me. Question God. It is His way of doing things.

Superman Talmadge

When my little hero, Talmadge was all of eight years old, he thought he was Superman. In school, the little fella used to sit at his desk, daydream about sailing gracefully out the window, rescue his "Lois" and cradle her up and down Second Street so that all the other little boys would say "Superman Talmadge done done it again."

But the boys would never say 'Superman Talmadge done done it again' because Superman Talmadge had never done it in the first place and his Lois, a chubby little dumpling of eight and a half was never in need of rescue.

But you cannot stop the dreamer.

One day after school, Talmadge swaddled his neck with his daddy's only sheet and paraded up and down the streets.

Trailing closely, were the mocking little boys. Second Street. But the boys were not impressed. "You ain't no Superman," they chorused.

"I is,"

"You ain't…. not."

"I is so."

"You ain't not, neither."

"I is so, too."

"You ain't not!! Y'can't lift no train!!"

"I ain't the kind of Superman that can lift no train. I'm the kind'a Superman that can fly."

"We ain't never seen you fly nowheres."

"That's cause y'all ain't been lookin'."

"We lookin' now, superman Talmadge," they said, again mocking the word *Superman.*

Now, that was a challenge and Superman Talmadge could ill afford to let it pass. And he didn't. Like a little Pied Piper, he led the string of boys from Berry Street to Beach Street, across the tracks, around Bootsie Boyd's, the Huylers and B.J.'s house, down Mr. Marshall's and Coleman's alley, across Mr. Bucknight's and Lonnie Johnson's yard, over the McCall's and Nettles' fence and finally home. He halted the procession in his backyard and pointed a finger up to the attic window. "Keep y'eyes on that there window right up there, Y'unnerstan?"

"We unnerstan," they said.

Minutes later Superman Talmadge appeared in the attic window. Two of the little boys cheered, the rest did not. But it did not affect the man of the hour. He stood there proudly, his cape blowing in the gentle breezes of spring. One of the little boys glumly looked up and said, "Anybody can stan' in a attic window with a sheet on."

"I ain't stannin' in a attic window with a sheet on, I'm stannin' in my super-secret hidin' place with my super-secret cape on."

"Don't look like it to me," said on the boys who had cheered.

"Yeah!" hollered another. So far, you ain't doin' nothin' but stannin' in a attic window with a sheet on. Anybody can do that."

"Yeah. C'mon, fly—if you gonna fly"

How far y'gonna fly, Supe?

"You gonna find out when I fly!"

"Give us a idea," piped the main disbeliever.

"I'm gonna fly – "I tell you guys, I'm gonna fly from here to the sky!"

"Well, hurryup so's I can run home an' tell my momma to watch."

"I ain't flyin' to suit your momma!"

"So far," chirped a voice, "you ain't flyin to suit nobody. You just stannin' up there with a sheet on. Anybody can do that.... "C'mon, fly IF you really gonna fly."

"Yeah, Supe. Don't keep us waitin'!"

Swept away, they all joined in: "C'mon, superman Talmadge, fly! Fly, Talmadge, fly...fly! Be a *real* Superman! Fliiiee...!! Fliiieeee...!!"

To halt the barrage, Superman Talmadge shot his arms out from his sides.

The boys fell silent. And for a moment, so did the man of the hour.

Suddenly, he stood tall – as rigid as he could. Then, for all the world to see, he jumped. And for all the world to hear, from the attic to the ground, Talmadge yelled: "SHAZAMM!!!

--It was over.

When the ambulance growled to a stop the attendant hopped out and elbowed his way through the circle of little onlookers, who had fallen ever so quiet. He knelt beside the fallen one. He knew better, he knew much better, but with care he asked, "Are you alright, sonny?"

Superman Talmadge slowly open his eyes and looked up at the attendant. His face glistening with beads of sweat his eyes filled with hope, he parted his lips with pained effort. His voice was beneath a whisper. "Tell me somethin', mister, "D-d-did I… Did-d-d d I fly?"

The attendant shook his head. "No, son. No, you didn't fly. Little boys weren't meant to fly. Little boys aren't meant to fly. Little boys are meant to do many things. But flying is not one of them."

One of the little boys, anxiously looking around for support while tugging on the kneeling man's arm, sharply disagreed. "But he did fly, mister! …He flew! Guys, didn't we see Supe fly?"

"Yeah, we saw 'im," they agreed, almost in unison, and almost to each other. "We saw 'im fly. Superman Talmadge *flew*. All'a us guys saw 'im fly. We did! Didn't we see 'im fly, guys?"

"Yeah!" they chorused loudly, and vigorously nodding their heads to each other. "Talmadge flew! He did, he did, he did!! Superman Talmadge really, really flew!!"

Arms draped around each other, skipping, hopping, and cheering, they exploded in exultation – almost steppin' on their hero. But that was all right with him. From the corner of his eyes, he looked at them for a quiet moment, then closed his eyes for the last time. Superman Talmadge was smiling his brightest smile.

He knew, even as you and I should know that you cannot stop the dreamer. Oooh, it is all so fascinating -- everything is, the world is. It is ever so magical.

And truth be told, one does not know if one is the dreamer or if one see's one who is acting at the behest of the "original" dreamer... nothing is ever done alone.

I say that because I thought I heard the real dreamer – I thought I heard the original dreamer say to no one in particular, "I think I'll wait down here for a little while longer, then I'll go back up there... and I'll have that little fella try his flight all over again... Only this time, we'll do it together...   And don't worry. -- I'll be there to catch him... just in case.

Thank You....

I thank you One and All.

ADDENDUM E

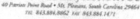

CONGRESSIONAL MEDAL of HONOR FOUNDATION
40 Patriots Point Road • Mt. Pleasant, South Carolina 29464
TEL 843.884.8862 FAX 843.884.1471

April 1, 2009

Mr. James McEachin
██████████████████

Dear Old Soldier:

On behalf of America's Medal of Honor recipients, particularly those who attended the dinner in New York, their exclusive Society and the Congressional Medal of Honor Foundation, thank you for your performance at last week's *Circle of Honor* dinner. You mesmerized our guests with your short performance and stimulated them to think carefully about your words on freedom and those whose sacrifices make it possible to live the way of life we do.

The Circle of Honor dinner is very important to the Foundation because it provides the resources that enable us to help perpetuate the rich legacy of the Medal of Honor. There is simply no more suitable place than the Stock Exchange to meld together the premier symbol of global free enterprise and those who represent in a profound way the men and women whose courage, sacrifices, and selfless service have played such an important part of preserving the freedoms we enjoy as Americans.

James, as you probably know, more than 60 percent of those who have been awarded this prestigious Medal since the beginning of World War II received it posthumously. President Franklin Roosevelt once said, "Those who have long enjoyed such privileges as we do today, forget in time that men have died to win them." Our initiatives not only reinforce the spirit of freedom that so many Americans have fought and died for, they help perpetuate the legacy of the Medal of Honor and the recipients who have contributed so much to our nation and its way of life through their selfless acts of courage.

As a small expression of appreciation for you taking the time to help make this year's *Circle of Honor* dinner very special and memorable, we have enclosed a copy of *Medal of Honor: Portraits of Valor Beyond the Call of Duty* signed by the recipients who attended the dinner. We hope you will cherish it as a valuable keepsake. Again, thanks....we wish you the best.

Most respectfully,

Robert Lewis Howard
Robert L. Howard
Society President

Nick Kehoe
Nicholas B. Kehoe
Foundation President

...rtraits of Valor Beyond the Call of Duty (signed)
...erpetuating a legacy of courage, sacrifice and patriotism
www.cmohfoundation.org

Age 15, me and my Mother

A FINAL POSTSCRIPT

I had to move on before the wheels of the chariot turned away from me. Already I believe the angels have sent signals to alert me for instance, in writing all hours of the night I often get chills over some of my memories and thoughts that I have. I am mesmerized by them. Korea – or more accurately -- the creek -- is never distant from my mind. I can sometimes hear the bullets at odds with my steel helmet. I am transfixed. Sometimes I am a bit moist-eyed and almost like in a sleep-walk, I will get up and go to my crowded desk to write about my experiences. Unable to remain in bed, and no longer covering up, I have been drawn to the heater, and I've been warmed, but burned. When I talked to my VA Doctor, Dr. Wendal Ching, I felt compelled to tell him about the heater, many nights I am quick to turn it on, straddle it, and, at times I keep it turned on high. Most times and in a matter of minutes my thighs will become overheated. In fact, they burn, but I am so focused on what I am writing I can hardly move and its only later that I realize the full gravity of the predicament. Extreme? For sure. But I took cell phone pictures of the last episode. I submit them here.

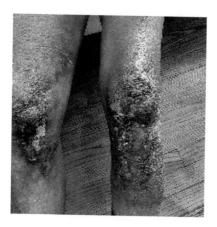

ABOUT THE AUTHOR

James McEachin is a Silver Star, Purple Heart veteran of the Korean War, an accomplished actor, and an award-winning author. Known as "Jimmy Mack" in the music industry, McEachin was a producer, songwriter, and eventually owner of the record label Mack IV best known for the doo-wop group, The Furys. Because of his long-held moniker in the industry, some speculate James McEachin to be the *Jimmy Mack* Martha (Reeves) and the Vandellas cried for in their hit song.

McEachin, having appeared in nearly 200 movies and television shows, is perhaps best known for his roles on *Perry Mason*, *Matlock*, *Play Misty for Me*, *First Monday*, and his NBC series *Tenafly*. He has authored six novels, multiple screenplays, and his one-man play, entitled *Above the Call; Beyond the Duty* which opened at the Kennedy Center in Washington D.C. The two-hour play has been seen in places as far away as Kuwait.

In 2005 McEachin was appointed a US Army Reserve Ambassador and spent his free time speaking to soldiers, veterans, and America. In late 2006 he produced the film-short *Old Glory*, a film short for the soldier, veteran, and patriot in us all.

He continues to speak for the veterans who may no longer have a voice to speak for themselves.

Currently he is in discussion with two production companies regarding his award-winning novel, *Tell Me A Tale*.

LITERARY WORKS BY JAMES MCEACHIN

Tell Me A Tale: A Novel of
the Old / Book

Farewell to the Mockingbirds
/ Book

Pebbles In the Roadway:
Tales and Essays; Bits and
Pieces / Book

The Heroin Factor / Book

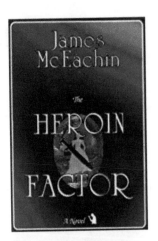

Say Goodnight to the Boys in
Blue / Book

The Great Canis Lupus /
Book

AUDIO AND VIDEO WORKS BY JAMES MCEACHIN

Pebbles In the Roadway:
Tales and Essays; Bits and
Pieces / CD

VOICES: A Tribute to the
American Veteran Old / CD

Old Glory / DVD

Old Glory Soundtrack / CD

Above the Call; Beyond the Duty: A one-man, one-act play